KIDS
HAVING
KIDS

KIDS
HAVING
KIDS
THE UNWED TEENAGE PARENT

BY JANET BODE

FRANKLIN WATTS
NEW YORK | LONDON | TORONTO | SYDNEY
1980

Library of Congress Cataloging in Publication Data

Bode, Janet.
Kids having kids.

Bibliography: p.
Includes index.
SUMMARY: Discusses the increased frequency,
causes, problems, and repercussions of teenage
pregnancy and parenthood.
1. Youth—United States—Sexual behavior—Juvenile literature. 2. Pregnancy, Adolescent—United
States—Juvenile literature. 3. Adolescent parents—United States—Juvenile literature. 4. Unmarried mothers—United States—Juvenile literature.
[1. Youth—Sexual behavior. 2. Pregnancy. 3. Adolescent parents. 4. Unmarried mothers. 5. Unmarried fathers] I. Title.
HQ27.B62   301.41'75   79-26321
          ISBN 0-531-02882-8

CONTENTS

TO CAROLE MAYEDO

ACKNOWLEDGMENTS

I want to thank the following people for their continuing support and encouragement: Barbara Althoff, David Chesnick, David Fechheimer, Jeannie Dougherty, Audrey Kavka, Robin Lafever, Michael Mendelson, Jean Naggar, David Rich, Barbara St. Germaine, Austin Scott, Catherine Sollecito, and Terry Tomaselli. The staff members at the San Francisco Planned Parenthood, especially Chris Grumm, deserve much praise for their help and cooperation. A special word of appreciation goes to my family—my father and step-mother, Barbara, Carolyn, Tony, and Judy—for their love and understanding.

This book would not have been possible if the many teenagers I interviewed had refrained from speaking openly and honestly. I sincerely thank all of them.

KIDS
HAVING
KIDS

CHAPTER 1
TEENAGE SEXUALITY AND PREGNANCY— THROUGH TIME AND AROUND THE WORLD

Sex. Stop and think about that topic. What images enter your mind? Now think about pregnancy. What mental picture does that word create? In your mind, you know that having sex can lead to pregnancy. Sometimes you don't connect the fact that if YOU are the one who is having sex, there's a chance YOU could get pregnant or, if you're male, cause a pregnancy.

The pictures don't stop there. A pregnancy has a beginning and an end. The next scenes could include an abortion, a miscarriage, or maybe a child's birth, and a final view of you as a young parent. You, the American teenager, aren't the first to discover sex. This highest form of physical intimacy has been around since time began. And pregnancy—planned or unplanned—has always been a possible result of having sexual intercourse.

There's nothing wrong, bad, or dirty about sex. It's just as true that pregnancy isn't a sin. We all need and want to be close to others. We need human contact, to touch, embrace, and feel secure. We need to love and be loved in return. All of these desires are completely normal. The problems begin when you start fooling around without considering that sexual activity must be combined with knowledge, maturity, decisions, and responsibility. The problems become even greater when you don't admit that having sex can cause an unwanted pregnancy. As one teenager said, "There's more to sex than just doing it."

Dr. Mary Calderone, president of the Sex Information and Education Council of the United States (SIECUS), has spent years helping people understand their sexual nature. When talking to teens Dr. Calderone stresses that "sex is natural to being human and part of being born human." She continues with this advice. "There's another part of being human—your mind. You must make choices. Ask yourself what kind of a sexual person do I want to be? How will I know I'm ready to accept the responsibility of actual physical, sexual intercourse? Decisions about sex are no different from any other important life decisions. They demand your best thinking, your highest morality, your deepest sense of responsibility. No one can make these decisions for you. You're the one living inside your body."

From cave-dweller days to this moment, societies have made rules according to their definition of accepted sexual behavior. People learn those rules consciously and subconsciously. They sense what happens if they break them. But throughout history social standards and individual behavior haven't always been the same.

Different cultures have had different standards concerning what adults should and shouldn't do sexually. They have also had rules for the younger community members—the people your age—to follow. Often those standards of behavior were related to religious beliefs, how much was known about reproduction, and the needs of the community.

If you'd been living in the primitive times from about 20,000 to 10,000 B.C., you'd have found that those people allowed each other a lot of sexual freedom compared to now. They could pretty much do what they wanted. No one worried about unplanned pregnancy, because they hadn't figured out that conceiving a child was what could happen after you had sexual intercourse. The primitive person thought babies appeared from other causes. Some said it was magic. Others felt that the moon had the mystical power to create life. Many cultures gave credit to their fertility ceremonies—rites for helping a woman become pregnant.

People didn't live very long in primitive times. A woman who had had ten children might see only two survive to adulthood. Many of the kids died at birth or within the first year of life. Because of that the people wanted to do everything they could to make sure their race continued. As they began to learn the real reason a woman got pregnant, they did a lot of things to enhance their fertility. If you were fertile that meant you'd have more kids.

So they carved fertility idols. They made drawings and wall murals of sexual events. On special occasions they performed songs and dances to please their gods and goddesses so they'd be rewarded with increased fertility. All of these activities were a big part of their religion. Many groups saw their own fertility and that of their crops as the same thing. For that reason planting and harvesting the fields took on extra importance. During those seasons there were celebrations, drinking, and praying. There were also sexual activities. They hoped their complete world would be bountiful and multiply.

If you moved on in your study of different sexual rules, you would find more examples of the intertwining of encouraged sexual behavior with religious practices. Maybe you would read about the pyramid builders who populated Egypt from 4,000 to 1,000 B.C. Or you could review information about the Babylonians of the same era. Their religions were all widely known for their permissive attitudes toward sex. It was accepted that men would attend temple ceremonies with gifts for their gods and goddesses. The priestesses would receive them, and in exchange for the presents they'd have sex with the worshippers. Many of these traditions were carried over to ancient Greece and eventually to Rome.

When it came to sex, people of the Jewish faith followed the laws delivered to them by Moses. Husbands and wives were supposed to be monogomous and faithful to their partners. Beyond this were other laws and practices regarding sex intended to sanctify physical union within marriage.

Then nearly two thousand years ago Christianity began. For a while the early members weren't too strict about sex. The ties to their ancestors were still fairly strong. Their theory was you shouldn't be ashamed to mention or experience sex. God hadn't been ashamed to create it. Those of the Jewish faith shared this belief. But attitudes and practices started to change.

The Christian leaders began denouncing all types of sexuality as the essence of evil. They said non-Christians were heathens. Those other religions were impure—those associated with sex and sexual activities. It was a Christian duty to introduce chastity and decency into religious worship. This hadn't been a major part of any religion before.

If you've ever grumbled about the moral rules now, they're nothing compared to what was happening by the third century A.D. The religious leaders had begun concentrating on other spiritual values, so the lawmakers and rulers took over where they thought the church wasn't being strict enough. Having no sex at all was considered the best way to live. If you wanted to have sex—and only with your spouse—it was okay except on Sundays, Wednesdays, and Fridays, plus 40 days before Easter and Christmas.

By the time of the Renaissance, about the fourteenth to the seventeenth century, people decided enough was enough. Their curiosity about the topic started again. They acknowledged the beauty, joy, and wonderment of sexuality and the human body. Not everyone had this attitude, though. Some famous experts on anatomy apologized to their colleagues, patients, and students for describing the sexual organs. Sometimes they ignored them entirely, as if sex didn't exist.

The inhabitants of the Western World gradually relaxed their attitude as they edged into the eighteenth century. This was an age of exploration. While their ships circled the globe, Europeans at home revealed an even stronger curiosity about sex and a desire to figure out what it was all about. The religious leaders and royal families became worried about the non-Christians in other areas of the world and about their citizens at home. They wanted to spread the word of their way of living and simultaneously convert others to Christianity. To do this work, missionaries followed on the heels of the adventurers. When they went to distant lands, they were horrified by the variety of sexual activities they witnessed. Christian and European rules weren't followed everywhere.

Codes of moral conduct loosened and tightened in turn as the years passed. Finally Queen Victoria of England came to power in 1837 and reigned until her death in 1901. The sexual standards that came to be identified with her and that era were harsh and far-reaching. Of course, there should be no sex except within marriage. In addition, many more rules were put forth that were never mentioned in the Bible. For women sexual experiences or even feelings were something to put up with. Sex should never be fun or pleasurable, especially if you were female. Not only was masturbation a wicked sin, but it also caused a wide range of ailments from insanity to blindness. Some parents warned their children it made hair grow on the palms of your hands, and that it could also cause acne. Just having sexual thoughts was evil. And on and on. Some of these ethics remain in our century, but slowly more people have been reevaluating them.

Meanwhile, in other areas of the world, different cultures were following their own rules. Some were more lenient toward sex than others. In certain parts of Africa, like western Kenya and Malawi, sexual activities before marriage were and are permitted. Even having a child at a young age is condoned. That proves a woman's fertility and makes her more desirable as a wife.

In parts of east and south Africa things are tighter. Throughout the centuries many cultures there have absolutely forbidden any sexual relations before the circumcision of the males, or some kind of initiation rite around the age of twelve. After those take place, teenagers are given instructions about sex by the older community members. The teens learn how to avoid penetration and to use withdrawal to try to prevent pregnancy. In several south African tribes the expectant mother is punished if a pregnancy does occur. She may be kicked out of her community or forced to marry the father even against her will. Sometimes an abortion is performed. But under dangerous conditions. A few groups require that the new baby be killed at birth.

For hundreds of years single individuals of the opposite sex were routinely separated in China. To make sure of minimal contact, and to avoid surprise pregnancies, females were assigned to "girls' houses" for part of the day and to sleep at night. The adults had decided this was the way to stop any fooling around before marriage. This is still true today in some rural parts of China.

After reading this short survey of rules for sexual behavior, you realize there are a lot of differences. What one culture considers all right, another says is wrong. What is okay during one century, becomes unacceptable during the next.

What's happening now to make matters more confusing is that people and nations around the world are in a period of transition and turmoil. This is a troubling time to live in. The old rules are falling away, but we haven't come up with a good set to take their place. For decades those of us in the Western countries have been raised with the guideline that when it comes to sex it should only happen within marriage. Sex should be saved for one person alone—your spouse. There's nothing wrong with this rule. Many who follow it have found stability, comfort, and happiness. But for a variety of reasons, more and more people at younger and younger ages are disregarding it.

There are a combination of related factors that are contributing to this worldwide increase in teen sexual activity and pregnancy. They all have to do with change—change in people and in moral values. These are among the main factors: the movement of people to cities; adult confusion about their own sexual activities; the new concept of adolescence as a special period between being a kid and becoming a grown-up; the delay in time before getting married; and for females, starting to menstruate when they are younger. Let's look a little more closely at how these factors work together.

Until this century the majority of the world's population lived in rural or small suburban areas. Communities were closely knit. There was heavy pressure to follow the appropriate rules in all parts of your life. If you didn't, both your family and the others in your neighborhood would make you know you'd behaved in a wrong manner. Now more people are moving to large cities in search of a better life. They are leaving their relatives and old friends behind. One isolated family can't put the same amount of force on their kids to guarantee that they will go along with the traditional ways of acting. The result is that even when parents try to instill certain ethics in their children, they have a harder time convincing them of their value. An individual parent's words have less impact than those of an entire culture.

And what about the adults? Many of them are as perplexed by the changing moral values as you may be. While they may teach, and sometimes preach, the rule of sex only with a marriage partner, not all of them toe the line themselves. Especially in the United States, but in other countries as well, the total family structure is standing on wobbly legs. The divorce rate is soaring. Many adults can't agree on the correct sexual conduct for themselves, let alone on how you—the younger generation—should be instructed when it comes to this topic. It's becoming more prevalent for you to hear the mixed message, "Do as we say, not as we do."

At one time teen sexual activity and pregnancy were not of much concern for an unusual reason. Before the turn of the century no one paid special attention to the years between thirteen and nineteen. Individuals' lives were simply divided into two categories. First you were a child, then you became an adult. A girl was considered a woman when she started to menstruate. A boy reached manhood at a certain age, such as twelve, or was initiated into the adult world after going through some type of ceremony. Kids followed kids' rules and grown-ups adhered to their own. If society considered you an adult at twelve, or thirteen, or fifteen, you didn't have much time to break the rule of little sexual contact.

Now increasing numbers of cultures have accepted the idea that our bodies, minds, and emotions slowly move through stages of development. You don't turn into an adult overnight. So we've added a new, special time category—the adolescent years. What's forgotten is that those specific, sexual feelings people start experiencing during that time haven't disappeared. They remain present. It's just that society defines you as in-between being a child and an adult. And sex, they say, is off limits to you unless you're a married adult.

In many societies sex before marriage wasn't always thought to be a big deal for another reason. People got married when they were quite young. If you were husband and wife by twelve or thirteen years old, that didn't give you much time to have sex beforehand even when it was okay. You weren't single long enough. The tradition of early marriages differs from country to country. At one time parents in India married off their daughters prior to their beginning menstruation. During this century that's changed somewhat, with the mean age for females when they marry rising from 12.8 to 16 years old.

Experts estimate that currently 40% of all women in Africa are wives by the time they reach nineteen. For Asia, nearly 30% have taken the step by that age. In nations like Bangladesh, Nepal, and Pakistan, more than 70% are married by their twentieth birthday. In the more industrialized countries marriage is often postponed until the females are older. In the Soviet Union only 9% of the women under twenty have become wives. The figure is 7% for those in Europe. In the Americas about 15% of the female population has walked down the aisle by the age of nineteen. People are discovering that the longer you delay marriage, the more likely you are to stop following the rule of virginity until your wedding night. And with sex comes the chance of an unplanned pregnancy.

There is another factor that has contributed to the high pregnancy rate. Before a young woman begins to menstruate, she's very unlikely to become pregnant. Today females everywhere are starting their periods at earlier ages than in previous generations. That means there are more years during which they can become mothers. One hundred years ago half of European women didn't begin menstruating until they were about fifteen. Now half start by twelve years old. According to Sheri Tepper, a Planned Parenthood official, one third of all American females have their first period at or before eleven. Experts state that the average age is dropping by about six months per decade. That's a drastic change. Doctors believe that a combination of better nutrition and wider availability of good health care have caused this to happen.

All of these factors are found around the world. The result is that sex and pregnancy before marriage are increasing globally. It's happening in Great Britain, Sweden, West Germany, Australia, Japan, and elsewhere. The big difference in the United States is that our birth rate—the number of births per 1,000 females —for adolescents is among the highest of any developed nation. Only in Bulgaria, East Germany, Rumania, and New Zealand is the number of births among young women higher. The percent of American teenagers giving birth is even greater than it is in some Third-World nations such as Tunisia and East Malaysia. Worldwide a total of 13 million females under the age of twenty gave birth in 1977. If you add those who had abortions or miscarried, the final tally of those who became pregnant is still larger.

This all boils down to a global concern about teen sexual activity and pregnancy. Nations are working individually and together to try to meet this concern. After reading this overview of the topic, it's time to focus on you and what's happening in this country.

CHAPTER 2
STATISTICS ARE HUMAN BEINGS

What are the facts about teenage sexual activity and pregnancy? To begin with, you've got a lot of company if you're between the ages of fifteen and nineteen. Rounded off there are 21 million of you in the United States alone. Stretched out head to toe you'd circle the equator nearly three times. It's estimated that 7 million of the males and 4 million of the females have had sexual intercourse. Look around your classroom. Assuming it is a perfect reflection of the nationwide statistical picture, if there are twenty-one students, more than half of you would be having sex—seven of the young men and four of the young women. Ten of you would still be virgins.

No matter which category you're in, you should think about the following information. If you're already having sex, you have a responsibility to yourself and others to know as much as possible about the complete picture. Those of you who are adhering to the rules of society and are waiting until marriage will still be better prepared for the future.

You may call sexual intercourse "getting it on," "doing it," "getting over," "tripping," or "scoring." The words you use don't change this result. In any one year, one out of every four teen females who are having sex will become pregnant. Each year there are a million pregnancies in this age range. The vast majority are unplanned and unwanted. Planned Parenthood officials report that when it comes to unmarried teens as few as 10% of the pregnancies are intentional. With young married couples, more of the babies are planned, but certainly not all of them.

Researchers at Baltimore's Sinai Hospital spent six years studying the issue of adolescent pregnancies. They interviewed about 400 young mothers, their partners, their kids, and their parents. Then they talked to them again, one year and five years after childbirth. To compare their lives with those of teenagers without children, over 300 of their classmates were also interviewed.

Just 9% of the expectant mothers said they didn't use birth control on purpose, because they wanted to get pregnant. For the other 91% the news of their pregnancy was greeted with astonishment and disbelief. A further emotion, at least in the beginning, was despair.

When they were asked how they felt about becoming pregnant, only one out of five said that she was happy. Even these young women hedged in their responses. They described themselves as "sort of happy" and they felt "kind of good." Three quarters of those interviewed stated they wished they hadn't become pregnant. Half of them hid the fact from their parents for several months. Generally they didn't really tell them. Their mothers found out about it from some other source or figured it out on their own.

As their pregnancies progressed, some started feeling a little better. Still, less than a third said they were "very happy." Those whose attitudes had changed were usually those who had married. Just 3% of the pregnancies occurred within marriage. By the time of birth, almost 25% were new wives as well as young mothers. These women, too, expressed doubts and worries about their double roles.

I talked with more than 100 teens who became pregnant. Some live in large cities. Others come from suburban and rural areas. This event that should cause joy, too frequently had the opposite effect. The potential parents were extremely upset. In most instances, only when the child was conceived after marriage did the young couple say they were pleased about the situation.

Ann is fifteen, comes from a middle class background, and resides in a sprawling suburban community. When her pregnancy was confirmed she told me, "I felt really shocked and ashamed. I never thought I'd be the one to get pregnant."

A different reaction was mentioned by Beth, also fifteen. "Believe it or not, I got pregnant my first time having intercourse. When I found out I was very angry at myself for being so stupid. I kept thinking, this is not happening to me. But it was."

When Nan was sixteen she became pregnant. After missing a period she felt "worried, upset, and didn't know what to do." Nan explained, "I was scared to death. I cried and cried. What would my boyfriend say? Should I tell my parents? It was a heavy trip when it all came down."

Jackie's feelings were much more positive. She

and Patrick had been going together for over a year. At seventeen she learned she was pregnant. "We were really in love," she said. "Getting pregnant speeded up our marriage. I felt nervous, but then the whole thing blew me away. I was so happy and excited."

Look at the statistics again. One million teen pregnancies a year. For 14% of the young women decisions are unnecessary. They are among the 140,000 who miscarry. While this is hard to take physically and emotionally, their lives aren't as changed as the others. But they find that a miscarriage can't be kept a complete secret. They need medical attention to make sure that everything is all right. Sometimes there are serious complications.

Violet, sixteen, was unmarried and pregnant. She had a miscarriage. The hemorrhaging was so bad that she had to go to a hospital and have blood transfusions. It took her several weeks to get back her strength and return to normal. Yet she and many others like her were glad about one thing. They didn't have to choose between having an abortion and having a baby. Those who had wanted to become pregnant were deeply grieved by the loss. Those who had no desire to be mothers at that age, found that relief was their main emotion.

One third of the pregnant teenagers, about 300,000, reject the immediate prospect of motherhood. For many different reasons that will be discussed later, they have abortions. About half of all the adolescents who obtain abortions are eighteen or nineteen years old; 45% are between fifteen and seventeen; and 5% are fourteen or younger. Teens account for a third of the total number of abortions performed each year. Planned Parenthood's Alan Guttmacher Foundation researchers estimate that an additional

125,000 teens want to have abortions, but can't obtain them.

By choice or circumstance approximately 600,000 adolescents give birth each year. The number of children conceived outside of marriage is on the rise. At least to start out with, it's hard for any unmarried person to be delighted when learning she's pregnant. Single mothers of all ages, but especially those in their teens, are put down by many people. About one third of all teen births—200,000—are to single mothers. Another one sixth are pregnant on their wedding day. The remaining 300,000 women conceive after marriage.

Although the birth rates for older teens have gone down slightly over the last few years, the decline hasn't been as great as that for women in their twenties and thirties. Another fact that's bothering people is that younger sisters are now getting into the act. The figures for those fourteen years old and younger have climbed sharply.

One fifth of the 8 million thirteen– and fourteen–year–olds have had sexual intercourse. Each year 30,000 pregnancies occur to females in that age group. A little less than half of these pregnancies result in live births. The rest are ended by abortion or miscarriage.

According to the *Population Bulletin,* a publication of the Population Reference Bureau, Inc., the teen birth rate is higher among ethnic minorities than among whites. For young women under fourteen the rate for nonwhites is five times greater. But the difference narrows with age. Among nineteen–year–olds, the minority rate is less than twice the white rate.

For example, out of a group of 1,000 minority females fourteen years of age, about 22 give birth. The figure for whites is not quite 4 out of 1,000. With sixteen–year–olds, 85 of every 1,000 minority women become parents at that age. It's 29 of 1,000 whites. During the last five years there's been a change in these statistics. The birth rates for young women over sixteen is decreasing for both groups at about the same percent. Rates for sixteen–year–olds have remained pretty steady for white teens, but have decreased approximately 10% among ethnic minorities. The big difference comes with the younger teens. Minority rates are falling, while white rates are increasing.

The Center for Health Statistics has calculated that in 1975 nearly 1% of all fifteen–year–old females had had at least one child. The same was true for 3% of sixteen–year–olds; 6% of seventeen–year–olds; 12% of those eighteen; and 20% of all nineteen–year–olds.

Statistics and percentages can be confusing. They also help you hide from the cold facts. When you clear out all the numbers this is what's up. Adult pregnancy rates—for those over nineteen—have been dropping for the last few years. Generally yours have been too, but not as much. Also the characteristics of those who become pregnant have been changing. It used to be that older teens from poor homes and troubled backgrounds were more likely to be the ones having sex and getting pregnant. Now more and more younger adolescents from middle and upper class backgrounds are joining in. For better or worse when a "problem" moves to the wealthier neighborhoods more people become concerned.

Another thing happens when you look only at numbers. You start forgetting that each statistic means that the lives of individual teens are involved. Their futures, and those of their children, are being altered. The physical and emotional toll is great. Few adults are left untouched, either. Some are learning from personal experience, because their sons and daughters have become young parents. Millions more are involved indirectly, yet it still makes quite an impact on them.

These figures translate into dollars and cents. A study by the Stanford Research Institute, published in 1979, shows that federal, state, and local governments paid out $8.3 billion in 1978 to pregnant teenagers and teen mothers. That money went for cash support payments, food stamps, social services, medical care, and other programs. Taxes were the source of that money. When cash becomes part of any situation, you start hearing demands that "something must be done!"

The course of the nation is in your hands. For that reason alone, you may find it worthwhile to examine the total scope of this issue. It is also possible that you may find yourself more directly involved in an unplanned pregnancy.

CHAPTER 3
WHY ARE "KIDS" HAVING KIDS?

Statistics and percentages don't answer the question why increasing numbers of American teens are becoming sexually active before their wedding night. They don't explain why more adolescents are becoming pregnant. Coming up with a concise list of answers is as easy as keeping a pet octopus in a box. The minute you think everything is covered, another tentacle-like reason slips out. Some are intertwined. Others overlap. Still others vary according to location. A few are contradictory.

The best we can do is to record some explanations. These are a summary of theories provided by teens across the country and results of scientific surveys. They're a starting point. You may be able to think of even more answers.

Everywhere you turn sex seems to be the message. It's in the air, on the movie screen, in the minds. Products from automobiles to zithers are sold with not so subtle hints that they'll increase your sex appeal. You come to believe that being sexually active is a sign of maturity, sophistication, and status. Sexual freedom and exploration are encouraged. There is direct and indirect pressure to go with those feelings, whether you're ready or not.

At the same time, large numbers of you say you think sex before marriage is wrong. Frank Furstenberg, Jr. reported the results of several studies in the July/August 1976 issue of *Family Planning Perspectives*. He found in his research and other projects that nearly half the unwed teenage mothers questioned "stated that it was very important for a woman to wait until marriage to have sex." And yet they hadn't followed their own convictions.

There are more opportunities to be sexually active than in previous generations. Now everyone either owns a car or has access to one. With a car come privacy and temptation. If you add drugs and/or drinking, even the strongest resolve often disappears.

It's not unusual for both parents to be out of the house for extended periods of time. Many families are headed by only one parent who is at work, running errands, or doing other necessary tasks. That leaves extra hours and locations available for getting together with friends. Even though a lot of you are instructed by your parents not to have people of the opposite sex over while they're gone, you consider disobeying them. Many do. With no adult around, will power can diminish. A warm embrace grows warmer until it leads to intercourse.

Another reason offered falls under the general heading of "Pressure and Rationalizing." Many females say they are persuaded or even coerced by males to have sex. Do any of these lines sound familiar? "If you love me, you'll prove it." "Everybody's doing it, so why won't you." "Once you turn on a guy, you've got to follow through." "Sex is no big deal. What are you afraid of?"

It's not all the young men's fault. Young women are coming up with variations of their own. Have you heard any comments such as these? "I don't want to lose my boyfriend. I have to go along with his desires." "If boys can do it, why can't we?" "I don't want to graduate from high school a virgin." "I want to keep up with the crowd." "It's natural, so how can it be wrong?"

Some teens presented this explanation. Sleeping with a person means your relationship together is important. It proves you're no longer a child, but have moved into the adult world. You become sexually involved for the same reasons that people do at any age —because of love, insecurity, the desire to be close to another individual, or simply out of curiosity. You may make up excuses for your motives. Sometimes things "just happen." After you take the first step, many find it hard or impossible to turn back. When you're no longer a virgin, there are fewer reasons to stop. That barrier, once crossed, can never be regained.

So you continue, and that's where more difficulties arise. Too frequently sexual intercourse isn't combined with an adequate method of birth control. Then you have the other set of statistics—the number of pregnancies among adolescents.

Why are there a million teen pregnancies yearly? While each case is unique, these responses were given often enough to show some basic causes. A blend of ignorance and misconceptions about birth control was revealed. Teens interviewed said they didn't know whether to laugh or cry about their erroneous knowledge. Here's just a sample of some misconceptions:

1. If you stand up while having intercourse, the female won't get pregnant.
2. Pregnancy can't occur until the female is at least 16 years old.
3. A woman never becomes pregnant the first time she has sex.
4. Pregnancy can only happen when both the male and the female have orgasms. (Of course some of you aren't even sure what an orgasm is.)
5. You're safe if you take a birth control pill right before you have intercourse.
6. It's impossible to become pregnant during a menstrual period.
7. If the woman goes to the bathroom after she's had sex, she's protected.
8. Vaginal hygiene sprays can be used as a birth control method.
9. If the male withdraws his penis just before he reaches a climax, the female won't become pregnant.
10. Jumping up and down or dancing right after sex, keeps pregnancy from occurring.
11. Spraying a soft drink into the vagina after intercourse halts pregnancy.
12. If you have sex infrequently, you won't get pregnant.

Not one of these statements is true. If you're sexually active and don't know the first thing about preventing pregnancy, there's a good chance you're going to wind up in that condition or causing it.

At times adults seem to be involved in a conspiracy of silence concerning the issue of sex. They believe that if they don't mention it, you won't figure out that it exists. By keeping you unaware of "where babies come from," you won't have any of your own until after you are married.

Alice, fourteen, said she was angry. She knew one reason why teenagers get pregnant. "It's adults' fault," she asserted. "Our parents think if we learn birth control information, then we'll be encouraged to go out and screw around. Don't they know that only if we have all the facts can we make choices of our own?"

Some adults have almost as limited knowledge of sex and reproduction as their children. Zero Population Growth came up with a test to check people's "contraceptive IQ." Among other items, they were asked when "a woman is most fertile (most likely to become pregnant)." Only 44% of the teens' fathers knew the correct response. Their mothers didn't do too well, either. Just 62% were right. For the record, 38% of the teens knew the answer.

In general, parents are very willing to answer any questions to the best of their ability. The problem is they frequently wait for YOU to bring up the subject. Perhaps they believe you're too young, would be embarrassed, or wouldn't have the foggiest notion of what they're talking about.

During the adolescent years communication between you and your parents or guardians is often at a low level. Many of you have difficulty discussing any issue with them, let alone one like sex! It results in a standoff. So where else could you go for the facts?

A natural place might be right in the classroom. It

could be one of the most important courses you'd ever study. Most teens think that would be a partial solution. Vickie is eighteen now. She began having intercourse at fourteen with fragmented knowledge of birth control. There are three daughters in her family. Each is intelligent, lively, and beautiful. Vickie and one of her sisters have had abortions. Vickie wishes there had been better guidance available.

"I started having sex so early," she explains. "I don't know why I felt I had to. I wish somebody had talked to me beforehand when I was younger. All my best friends have had abortions. One has had three, which is incredible to me. If all my friends have, then did practically EVERYBODY in high school?

"The health clinic didn't keep records of how old we are. My parents NEVER knew I had one and neither did those of any of my friends. We need help, counselors or someone coming into the schools and talking to us. We need classes that give us the straight facts. If only the adults realized."

In 1978, the first national conference on teenage sexuality and pregnancy was held in Atlanta, Georgia. More than 3,500 adolescents from almost every state met together to debate and examine these topics. Some completed a questionnaire on several issues including sex education in the schools. This large group reflected Vickie's sentiments. Almost unanimously those polled agreed that "all high schools (should) develop a full credit course in the freshman or sophomore year covering subjects such as male-female relationships, sexual responsibility, and infections you can get from having sex." The same held true when asked "Do you think information on birth control should be included in high school health programs?" The major difference of opinion revolved around the question, "Do you think actual birth control methods should be provided for students in high school?" About 60% believed they should be, while 40% said no.

There were also questions about whether masturbation, homosexuality, and venereal diseases should be discussed in these classes. The overwhelming majority felt these were necessary facets of any course on sex.

The Rev. Jesse Jackson, founder of Operation P.U.S.H. and a civil rights activist, attended that same conference. He told the audience, "Sex is too powerful to stay in the realm of superstition. Sex is too beautiful to be made ugly by ignorance, greed, or lack of self-control. We need to learn sex education in the first grade, the second, the third. We need to learn about our sex organs just as soon as we learn about our other organs."

Millions of other adults don't agree with that idea. They insist that sex education doesn't belong in the school system. Because adult opinion has more power than that of adolescents, they usually win this battle.

Planned Parenthood made a survey that showed only twenty-nine states and Washington, D.C., require health education courses in public schools. And just six of these states, plus the District of Columbia, make instruction on family life or sex education mandatory. Even where sex education is offered, only 39% of the schools include information about birth control. Nor do sex education classes alone seem to solve the problem. Carol Smith, a nurse-midwife and director of family life education at a California county hospital, discovered that while students may study birth control and anatomy, they don't always apply the information to themselves. That theory aside, hundreds of areas throughout the country either forbid or restrict sex education classes.

Invariably when teens were asked if they'd obtained any formal information outside of the home, they mentioned a single film on menstruation. This was generally seen, after parental permission had been given, by females in the sixth grade. Many adults consider that's all you need to know.

The rest of the topic ends up being treated like a hot potato. Some students have signed petitions requesting classes in sex education. They hand the issue to the principal who in turn says he'll have to take it up with the board of education. The board members don't want to deal with it, so they throw it over to a parents' organization, such as the P.T.A. Most parents rarely go to P.T.A. meetings, so the few who attend hesitate to make a decision that might upset those who are absent. Finally, the request becomes buried under a pile of papers.

A church or synagogue teen group might be another place to turn for information, but problems arise there as well. Attendance rates are fairly low. Adolescents who do participate report mixed feelings. Some of them say religious leaders often take one of three approaches. (1) Sex is never mentioned in a relevant, meaningful, or helpful way. (2) You're told, "Don't do it." (3) You're taught that "sex is evil and dirty, so save it for the person whom you marry and love."

Other adolescents say their religious youth programs are worthwhile. They are able to discuss their concerns with their peers and a trained adult. That person is neutral, but informed. Judgments aren't made. They find a positive balance of facts and a reinforcement of their spiritual beliefs.

A further logical source of information might be a family planning clinic, but again impediments are sometimes placed in your way. All large cities and many smaller ones have organizations such as Planned Parenthood, health centers, or hospital facilities that provide contraceptive instruction and birth control devices. Some have special hours for teens to make you feel more relaxed by being with others your own age. That sounds ideal until you confront these restrictions.

More than twenty states require parental consent before birth control devices are given to single females under eighteen, unless they have had previous pregnancies. Many of you don't want your parents to know you're sexually active, so you don't want to ask them to sign a permission form. Of the adolescents questioned by Zero Population Growth, 31% said they didn't obtain contraceptive services for that reason. Therefore they didn't practice any reliable method.

For others, parental consent isn't a problem. The Alan Guttmacher Institute released a study on this issue in October 1978. More than half of the teen women using contraceptives supplied by birth control clinics said their parents were aware of it. Only 11% of the 1,442 surveyed in ten states said they'd stop having sex if they needed parental consent to get birth control devices. Parental knowledge varied according to the area where the teens lived. Those more likely to tell their parents were in the Midwest and South. The ones less likely to inform them lived in the West and Northeast.

The study, based on written questionnaires, came from the responses of adolescents, who were seventeen years old and under, at 53 family planning clinics from New York to California. The number of teens using those services rose from about 690,000 in 1972 to almost 1.2 million in 1976. Even though that's a good sign, the Urban and Rural Systems Associates conducted a different study for the Department of Health, Education, and Welfare. Those researchers found that most clinics are "not reaching large numbers of sexually active teens, nor are they reaching them soon enough. . . ."

They discovered that several of the reasons for this go back to community attitudes toward teen sexuality and birth control. Many health centers are afraid to publicize their services, because parents might get upset. They could even force them to close. Other clinics have long waiting periods for an appointment and an additional wait once there. Some charge fees which make them too expensive for teens. Almost all of them are "female oriented." That means when a male goes in with his partner, let alone by himself, he's likely to feel as comfortable as if he'd walked into homeroom nude. Even when teens know about these clinics, many are confused about the range of help they provide.

Grace and Donald talked about their experiences in trying to find birth control information and advice. They're both sophomores and knew they weren't ready for marriage or parenthood. Although they had a basic knowledge on this topic, their difficulties didn't evaporate.

Grace faced these obstacles. "At first I didn't even know there was any place I could go to get birth control methods," she said. "I'd heard about a family planning clinic, but I didn't think that's what I wanted. I didn't want to 'plan a family.' I wanted NOT to plan one. Then I checked around to see if my mother would have to know if I went. Can't you imagine that conversation. 'Momma, Donald and I are having sexual intercourse. Would you sign this permission form so I can get the Pill?' That's my momma. She'd *die.*

"I called up the clinic and they said it'd be completely confidential. Still I felt funny. The hours weren't good for me. I'd have to talk to a lot of counselors first. I didn't know whether they'd charge me. I was scared. Then it all seemed so cold, calculated, and planned. I wasn't that kind of a girl. Maybe if birth control methods were easier to get without making us feel guilty or embarrassed, more of us wouldn't get pregnant. I sure wish I hadn't."

While you can bypass a clinic and buy several methods of birth control without a prescription, making the purchase isn't always simple. You may think it doesn't bother you until a salesperson comes up and says, "Can I help you find what you're looking for?"

Donald explained how he felt about this situation. He recalled, "I told Grace I'd take care of it. I'd use rubbers. I thought I was pretty together until I walked into the ol' drug store. I felt too stupid to buy them there. What if one of my mother's friends saw me. Things like that went through my mind. Then I went to the gas station. I'd seen a machine in the bathroom. Zipped in my money and whammy—nothing. Put in another 50 cents and the same thing. You think I was gonna go out and tell that man his machine didn't work? No way."

Consider what might happen if you had all the facts about birth control and there was no problem obtaining the best method for you. Not a single adult would have to sign an approval form. Everything would be free of charge. Would this make a difference? Would this drastically decrease the teen pregnancy rate? The answer—not necessarily.

At least a dozen studies have been completed to determine whether there's a relationship between knowledge of reproduction and birth control methods with their use. The researchers' published results include one by George Cvetkovick, Barbara Grote and their associates, called "On the Psychology of Adolescents' Use of Contraceptives," and Warren Miller's "Sexual and Contraceptive Behavior Among Young Unmarried Women." A summary of all these findings in plain language is this: Just because you know about contraceptive methods doesn't mean you'll use them.

Often you don't want to because it makes sex seem unspontaneous and unromantic. In Zero Population Growth's teen survey, 24% gave this reason. Others have intercourse very infrequently. It's a hassle to take the Pill daily, if your sex life is highly sporadic. Bringing a diaphragm, cream, foam, or jelly along on a date makes some of you feel guilty. You think you're more prepared than you might want to appear to be. Moral or medical objections were cited by 13% of the non-users.

The Baltimore Sinai Hospital study revealed another prevalent response. Many of those questioned simply believed they wouldn't be the one to "get caught." Teen females I spoke with offered another explanation. After being sexually active for a period of time without becoming pregnant, they thought they were somehow safe. They decided that withdrawal might really work. Or maybe they couldn't have kids.

What they didn't know is that if you start having intercourse when you're very young, you may not be ovulating yet. Therefore you can't get pregnant. Then as you mature the menstrual cycle regulates and the chance of conceiving increases. Combine that with a continuation of unprotected sex and pregnancy is generally the outcome.

Cathleen provided another typical reason. "I just never thought about if I was having intercourse without birth control I could get pregnant," she said. "Sometimes I don't take things seriously until it actually comes right down to it."

Tommy, sixteen, is a junior in high school in Detroit. His theories on teen sexuality and birth control are shared by many of you and confirmed by the experts. His ideas also give a male perspective.

"Listen, man, I used to be a heavy dude," Tommy began. "I'd rap with my buddies 'bout sports and scorin' with the chicks. You weren't a man unless you were screwin' around. I guess I had to prove something to myself, my friends. And I kept up with the best of 'em.

"We didn't have no big debates about birth control. We knew a guy could use rubbers. We've all heard about Pills, foam and stuff for the girls. There's even a clinic close-by. If you don't have much money, it's free. But facts are facts. We aren't gonna be the ones walkin' around with the big bellies. If chicks don't wanna get knocked up, it's their job to take care of it. That's life.

"Knowing 'bout birth control and where to get it doesn't make any difference. Ya' know why? 'Cause everyone's favorite methods are promises and luck. 'Don't worry, baby, I promise you won't get pregnant.' 'I promise everything'll be safe.' 'I promise I'll just stay inside you a lil' while.' And they buy it. 'Cause they don't want to think about it either.

"Luck? That's the name of the game in this country. You play the odds. Gamble. Take chances. Most times it doesn't run out. Girls do it, too. Guys ain't the only ones. Birth control is a hassle anyway. It spoils things. When you're out havin' a good time, ya' just don't stop and say, 'My dear, are you protected by some means of birth control? No? Then we must not have sexual intercourse. Or we must first go to the corner store and buy a contraceptive.' See, I even know the right words.

"Well, I pushed my luck too far. Judy got pregnant. She's an okay person, but I just told her, 'See ya' 'round.' She went to her girlfriends and they really got mad at me. I said it wasn't my fault. I didn't know how I coulda helped. I try to be more careful now. Think about the girls' feelings, too. But it's tough, man. Tough."

There are additional causes of pregnancy even when birth control is used conscientiously. Every method has a failure rate. For Pill takers from one to four out of every 100 will become pregnant. The diaphragm with cream, jelly, or foam doesn't always work. From two to twenty females will conceive a child. For the I.U.D., it's from two to six pregnancies per 100 women. The condom's failure rate is about three to thirty-six.

Two professors from Johns Hopkins University, John Kantner and Melvin Zelnik, have spent years researching teen attitudes and sexual activity. They conclude that even if unmarried teens consistently use birth control methods such as those mentioned above every single time they had intercourse, 500,000 would still become pregnant each year. At least 300,000 would give birth. The rest would have abortions or miscarry.

Pat, sixteen, learned she was the exception to the rule. Because she didn't want to become pregnant, she went to a clinic and got a prescription for the Pill. "I took them faithfully. I honestly never missed a day. I'd been on them for almost seven months, so I was convinced they did the job for me. After I found out I was pregnant, the doctor said they might not have been strong enough. I tried!"

Fertile women, teenaged and older, are learning this unfortunate fact. Each birth control device has some drawback—medical or emotional. Pills can cause blood clots, headaches, weight gains, and skin discolorations among other things. I.U.D. users report increased infections, uteral perforation, and so on. The diaphragm is a "natural" means, but many feel it is troublesome to use and detracts from love making. The other methods are much less reliable.

Although these problems plague informed women of every age, when teens become pregnant they seem to be blamed more than adults. But for all this negative information this is a more important point. The problems and failure rate of *no* birth control are the highest. If you have unprotected intercourse once a month, the risk of pregnancy is estimated at 2% to 4%. When it's more frequent, 80 to 90 females out of 100 could become pregnant over a year's time. There are only two methods that are guaranteed effective—no sex and sterilization.

A small but growing number of adolescents are becoming pregnant for a totally different reason. They are making a conscious decision to begin having babies at an early age outside of marriage. Why they do this varies. Some want to get out of the house, to be mature and independent. Others view it as a way to find love. Still others believe pregnancy and children are solutions to boredom, loneliness, or lack of direction. Rebellion and a means of retaliating against parents is a further explanation for this action. Tamarra and Cynthia are young mothers. They provided these background details.

Tamarra began, "I'd been fighting with my mother as long as I could remember. One of my girlfriends had a baby and it seemed like fun. I did drugs by the time I was ten. I started having sex at eleven. School was a drag. When you have a baby, you're an adult. Nobody tells you what to do or when to do it. That child was going to be my road to freedom and ticket to independence. So I quit school and had the kid, but motherhood is hard work. I sure didn't realize it would be like this."

Cynthia's experience has been better. When you meet her, she looks older than fourteen. She became pregnant at twelve, a mother by thirteen. "I wanted a baby," she told me. "I wanted someone to love and love me back. I didn't get the kind of love I expected out of my parents. They were always too busy for me. I used to try and get their attention. I wanted to yell, 'Listen to me. I need your help.' I deliberately started fooling around just to feel close to someone. I didn't like the sex part, but I did like being held.

"When I finally got pregnant, you know how my parents reacted? 'How could you do this to us?' 'What will the neighbors think?' All those years of needing them and their main worry was about their feelings and reputation. It isn't easy, but I'm a good mother. I truly love my child and I'm glad she's here."

Among all the statistics some people forget that 300,000 teen pregnancies occur after marriage. While not every single one is planned, most are. Kantner and Zelnik report that three fourths said their pregnancies were intentional. As young people, they have decided it is time to start their families. Even though relatives and friends might have encouraged them to wait, this is the couple's choice. There is never a completely right or wrong age at which to begin having kids for any married couple.

In this chapter you've read some of the causes of teen pregnancies: ignorance and misconceptions often caused by difficulties in obtaining accurate information and adequate birth control methods; not using preventive measures; birth control failure rates; and deciding to have a child no matter what others feel. Where there are impediments to gaining knowledge, they should be removed. You're going to have to work with adults in order to have that happen. Because they won't always lead the way, perhaps it's time you do.

CHAPTER 4
BEWARE OF
THE DOMINOES

Missed menstrual period. Nausea. Appetite loss or craving for a particular food. Tender or enlarged breasts. Frequent urination. Mood changes. All of these are signs of a possible pregnancy. Yearly more than one million teenage women experience these initial indicators.

Because most don't want to become pregnant, they try to explain away these effects they are noticing. Some remind themselves they've skipped a period before. It means nothing. The flu is going around. That's why they are getting sick. Exams are coming up. No wonder they're irritable. In case after case they put off having their suspicions confirmed or denied. Sally said her primary response was this. "I just wanted to stay in bed with the covers pulled over my head. I hoped if I ignored 'it,' it would go away."

Others contemplate dramatic solutions. They'll mysteriously vanish, or leap in front of a speeding truck. Vickie weighed her choices. One she called "my plan." A friend was going away to college. Vickie was welcome to move there with her. "I highly considered disappearing in the night," she said. "I didn't want to do anything about having a test. I knew I was pregnant. I just couldn't tell my parents." A few were excited. They wanted to find out as quickly as possible.

What should you do if you think you might be pregnant? Whether you're dismayed or delighted by the prospect, the first item on your agenda should be an immediate pregnancy test. For information and/or an appointment, call your local department of health, a hospital, family planning clinic, women's or student health center, Planned Parenthood, an abortion clinic, Birthright, or a private doctor.

The test, itself, is a simple procedure. All that's required is a blood or urine sample. The new Biocept G blood test, available at some medical facilities, is reportedly able to determine pregnancy as early as 10 days following conception. The more frequently used urine test is not accurate until 10 days after a missed period. Both tests provide results within a few hours or the next day.

Not every state permits teens to receive pregnancy tests without parental approval. If you want to keep it a secret from your family, ask a health worker about the policy in your town. Most will at least answer your questions without your having to tell your name. That means there's a little confidentiality for you. You should also check on the cost. The charge runs from nothing to over $20.

Diane, fifteen, dialed the number of the nearest hospital. It was private, charged $15, and her parents would have to sign a consent form. Diane explained, "In my state the only way you can get a test on your own is if you're married, already have a child, or are over sixteen. If that's not dumb, I don't know what is. I thought about lying, but I hate to do that. The woman I spoke to said, off the record, she'd suggest my going to a free clinic where they probably wouldn't hassle me. I took her advice and she was right. They didn't ask a bunch of questions. I just gave them a urine sample in a cup and called back in the afternoon."

Another option is purchasing a pregnancy test kit for approximately $10 from a drug store. This isn't a very good solution, because the instructions are complicated and the results are sometimes inaccurate. It is better than doing nothing.

Discovering you're pregnant brings out lots of emotions. This may be the first time you've had to evaluate your future plans and make such serious decisions. If you're single and pregnant, there are two choices: (1) having an abortion; (2) carrying the fetus to term. If you have the baby, you must decide whether it's best to raise the child yourself, place the baby in temporary foster care, have the infant adopted, or marry and raise the child with your husband.

Even when a baby is conceived within marriage, some are unintended. These young women, too, occasionally think about the alternatives. All these circumstances will be discussed in detail in later chapters.

Not only parents, but also health professionals, are extremely troubled by pregnancy among teens. This isn't just because of moral reasons. Equally important to them is the well-being of American youth and their possible offspring. Dr. Mary Calderone from SIECUS summarized that viewpoint. She's convinced that "no woman under the age of eighteen, rich or poor, married or not married, should ever get pregnant. The risks to the mother and baby are too great."

This information may be too late for you. If it is, remember this. You shouldn't feel alone when you're trying to figure out what to do. There are places to go for advice and guidance. Many adults care more than you might believe. If one counselor can't help you out, another might provide keys to solving your dilemma.

Diane continued with this recommendation. "Making the first call was the hardest. I felt scared and lost. After I found out I was definitely pregnant, they didn't say 'bye' and hang up. That staff was linked with other folks trying to help girls like me. No matter what I finally decide to do, I have names and numbers to contact. One individual can't do everything for me, but she can steer me in the right general direction."

Other good resources are also close at hand. You shouldn't dismiss any potential support and understanding from the man involved. Some react like creeps, but others don't. You could give him a chance. Teenagers I interviewed frequently mentioned a drawback to this. While they could be physically intimate with another person, they had a hard time talking together about their emotions and feelings. When it came to the news of a possible pregnancy, this was even truer.

An example is Sarah. She and Robb had been going together for about three months. After realizing she might be pregnant, she couldn't imagine telling him. She stated, "I can get it on with Robb, but I can't see myself discussing with him what's going on in my head."

The potential fathers had similar difficulties. Alex answered, "When Gwen told me she thought she was pregnant, I didn't know how I was supposed to act. Anything I suggested, she could misunderstand."

Even though you—the male—may have those

feelings, if you're asked for help you should try to provide it. The Rocky Mountain Planned Parenthood published a flyer on this entitled "She Will Always Remember You." It contains these statements for you to think about. "While she's sitting in the doctor's office, scared, waiting for the results of the test, she'll remember you.

"When the doctor tells her that she is pregnant, she'll remember you then.

"While she . . . tries frantically to find the money for an abortion . . .

"Or faces the disbelief and anger of her parents . . . she'll remember you.

"If you know that you'll always be remembered, is that what you want to be remembered for?"

For both the male and the female there's nothing wrong with turning to friends for suggestions. They may have faced the same situation. Don't discount your parents or guardians. Most teens interviewed said that once the first shock had passed, their parents were very caring. Connie was positive her mother would kill her. Alice had no doubt her parents would kick her out of the house. Instead, in both of these typical instances, their parents stood by them, offered sound advice, support, and reassurance. This could be true for you, too.

If you feel uncomfortable telling anyone, you still need information. You could go to a public library and check for books on adolescent pregnancy. Look at the bibliography in the back of this book for other sources of help in making decisions.

Ultimately you have to make up your own mind. To do this you may want to evaluate the possible complications and consequences of the alternatives. What about abortions? From the physical standpoint they are essentially safe, safer than carrying the fetus and delivering. With legal abortions only 1% lead to major difficulties. Problems are more likely to arise when the pregnancy is further along. Early abortions performed up to the twelfth week have the lowest rate of complications. During the thirteenth to fifteenth weeks the risks increase slightly. A late abortion—sixteen weeks or more—has the highest risk. Also, when you are four months pregnant or more many doctors hesitate or refuse to perform the procedure. Teens have more complications than adults because they wait longer before getting abortions.

For that very minute percent of cases where there are problems, these are the types of things that might occur. There could be excessive bleeding, an allergic reaction to the medication, or perhaps a minor infection. Occasionally some fetal material remains in the uterus. This is an incomplete abortion and rarely occurs. When it does, the tissue may be expelled spontaneously, or a dilation and curettage (D & C) may have to be performed to make sure you'll be all right.

There have been some instances where the uterine wall is perforated or pierced. Generally these cuts are small and heal on their own. Larger wounds can lead to trouble and additional surgery may be required to repair the damage.

In Chapter 5 you learn further details about this process—the cost, types, and emotional responses. You should consider these factors, too. While an abortion is a short, simple procedure, afterwards some women experience feelings of guilt, sadness, and regret. Most of them find their relief more than makes up for any bad reactions.

Because the majority of you decide to have the baby, these are some things of which you should be aware. There are many *possible* medical hazards for the expectant mother. The younger the female, the greater the danger.

These danger areas are caused by a combination of circumstances, many interrelated. Picture a line of dominoes. Knock over the first. It hits the next one, that topples the next. When a pregnancy is unplanned and unwanted, the young woman often delays having a pregnancy test. Pretending you're not pregnant isn't a solution and won't alter the results.

In reality you're subtracting from your options and adding to the possibility of complications. And the dominoes of hazards start falling against you. Without confirmation of a definite pregnancy, you're not going to begin seeing a doctor for prenatal care. When you don't have proper, prompt medical attention you're more likely to have difficulties.

Possible complications include bleeding during the first and last three months of the pregnancy. You may develop severe anemia as a result, a condition where the blood doesn't have enough red cells. This, in turn, can cause a lack of energy. Continually you feel tired.

Prolonged and difficult labor may occur. Adolescents interviewed said labor often lasted as long as forty hours. Have you ever had bad cramps during your period? This is merely a hint of what labor pains can feel like. Toxemia, an abnormal condition associated with the presence of poisonous substances in the blood, is another possible complication. Toxemia may also contribute to hypertension, extremely high blood pressure.

Miscarriage is another possibility. This happens in 10% of all teen pregnancies. While the probability isn't that high for an adolescent bearing her first child, it is much more likely when it's her second or third pregnancy. There's a 13% increased chance of death for teens aged fifteen to nineteen than for women in their twenties. The maternal mortality rate is highest for females under the age of fourteen. It's 60% more likely to occur than if they'd become pregnant in their twenties.

Sexual intercourse and pregnancy at an early age are associated with the occurrence of cervical cancer later on, even though other factors may be involved. On the positive side, research tends to indicate that women who have their first child before the age of eighteen have a decreased chance of developing breast cancer.

While you are young, your own body is still growing. You're in double trouble if you're in a growth spurt. Carrying a fetus at that time is more precarious for a body that hasn't completely matured.

Teens, just like other people, love junk food. Potato chips, candy bars, soft drinks, pizza, burritoes, french fries, and hamburgers aren't exactly what doctors call a balanced diet. A lifetime of poor eating habits makes matters worse. Bring on drugs, liquor, insufficient sleep, and what do you have—a bad outlook for your own health and your child's.

The younger you are, the greater the risks for the child. Young mothers have a higher frequency of giving birth before the nine month gestation is completed. These premature babies have low birth weights. That factor often contributes to congenital defects such as epilepsy, cerebral palsy, retardation, blindness, and deafness.

Dr. Janet Hardy, professor of pediatrics and co-director for the Center for Teenage Mothers and Their Children in Baltimore, Maryland, provided this documentation. She examined 525 kids born to mothers who were sixteen or younger at the time of delivery. When those children were four years old, 11% scored 70 or below on IQ tests, versus 2.6% of the general population. While 25% of all youngsters have IQs of 110 or above, the figure was only 5% for those born to these young women.

Among those I interviewed some mentioned that their offspring had physical and mental problems. This made the situation even more difficult for the young parents, to say nothing of their child's future.

If the infant doesn't weigh very much at birth, the chances of survival decrease. Children born to young mothers, as opposed to those in their twenties, are two to three times more likely to die, especially during the first month of life. Studies show that when the mother is fifteen years old or younger, 6% of the babies die in their first year of life. When adolescents are having a second or third baby, the child mortality rates increase again.

These possible results of pregnancy are not meant to alarm or frighten you. They don't have to apply to you. Although they occur in the minority of cases, they do happen occasionally and must be mentioned. Other consequences of early pregnancy and childbearing affect larger numbers of you. You have to think about your long-range goals and your ability to provide for a child.

Pregnancy and being a parent change many parts of your life. The domino effect can be seen again, because they are as interwoven as the causes of physical complications for young mothers and their babies. All these are affected—your future education, employment opportunities, income potential, marriage prospects and stability, further fertility, and the development of your children. While you can't completely control these variables, planning ahead often means you can overcome the stumbling blocks.

Continuing your education during pregnancy is a challenge. Many people think this is the primary reason teen women quit school. Kantner and Zelnik discovered that wasn't always true. In their study only one third of the female high school dropouts left because of pregnancy, but a different survey by J. Coombs and W. W. Cooley found a much higher percent in this category—one half to two thirds. Often these teenagers already had been held back a year or two. Others didn't like school, anyway, or wanted to find a job. When they learned they were pregnant, this was a final reason for leaving. Even good, conscientious students with career plans sometimes quit school, because of this new, time-consuming priority.

If you're pregnant you should think about the importance of a formal education. You could interrupt it for a while, and then return later. Studies show that many young parents who resumed their schooling proved to be excellent students. But once you stop attending classes, it's hard to go back. Experts estimate that only 20% of the young women who have a child before the age of eighteen complete high school. Among teen mothers fifteen and younger, just 10% ever graduate.

Then the next domino tumbles into place. Finding suitable employment is never easy. When you don't have a diploma and there is a child at home, you compound the problem. Two research projects—one conducted by Harriet Presser, the other by Frank Furstenberg—underline this fact. Being a young, unwed mother decreases your chances of future employment.

Inadequate education. Limited skills. Minimal, if

any, job history. "Sorry, we've nothing available for you," is the response you're likely to hear. Even when you can find something, day care for your child is an obstacle. Another domino falls.

How are you going to support yourself, plus a child? Before the baby is born you should be under a doctor's supervision. That costs money. The delivery is an extra expense. Some of you might qualify for federally financed health insurance, Medicaid, but others have to pay the bills themselves. And the amounts are high. After the birth, budgets may be even more strained.

Financial independence can be one of your biggest hang-ups. Too many people believe ALL adolescent mothers live on welfare. That's false. But if you can't find a job, or for those who are married, if your husband's salary is low, where is the money going to come from? Some unwed teens, as well as other single mothers, do periodically receive money from the federal government Aid to Families with Dependent Children (AFDC) program, which will be described later. Presser reported, in her 1975 New York City study, that half of the young parents were obtaining welfare, but that allowed three quarters of this group the flexibility to go back to school. Just because you become a mother at a young age doesn't mean you're destined to poverty. Your situation won't make things easier for you, but it's possible to beat the odds.

Another complex area of your life could be marriage. One researcher, Lee Burchinal, found that divorce and separation rates were two to four times higher for teen marriages, compared to those who married in their twenties. Paul Glick and Karen Mills discovered that when the husband was less than twenty and the wife less than eighteen, the chance of divorce was high for both blacks and whites. They were more likely to stay together when they had decent incomes. In Furstenberg's study, one fifth of the early marriages broke up within the first year, one third by the second. The total soared to 60% within six years. He stated, "By any standard, these rates are incredibly high."

Catherine Chilman writes in her book *Social and Psychological Aspects of Adolescent Sexuality,* that "the available studies indicate that marriage often makes the situation of the unwed adolescent mother worse, rather than better, unless the marriage has a sound social, psychological, and financial basis to begin with." Most don't. Furstenberg concluded that it doesn't really matter whether the young mother marries. "In time, she may be almost as likely as the unwed mother to bear the major, if not sole, responsibility for supporting her child."

Does that mean you shouldn't get married? Or, if you are married, that you'll probably get divorced? Yes and no. Again this is an individual matter. The statistics may be against you, but your name can be in the success column not among the failures. All marriages take time and attention. Worries about children, jobs, and money make things tougher. These problems are heavier the younger you are when you marry. Those are the facts.

Several studies highlight an additional trouble area. Almost half the teen mothers are pregnant again within three years of delivery. In Furstenberg's work, one in four become pregnant within 12 months. Many of those I interviewed said they soon stopped using adequate birth control methods. The result—another pregnancy. A few discovered they had conceived a second time within six months after the birth of their first child. Sometimes they had abortions because they knew they couldn't handle another baby so soon.

In general, women who give birth while in their teens have a larger completed family and tend to have their kids closer together. Those who have their first child at seventeen or younger will have 30% more children than women who don't begin their families until they are between twenty and twenty-four years old. For eighteen and nineteen–year–olds, the figure is 10% larger families than if they had waited a few more years.

An analysis in "Population Reports" mentioned this occurrence. The author felt young mothers might keep having children because they never develop other roles for themselves. There's been a lot of interest in this aspect—rapid childbearing. Now some experts believe that while this is one possible explanation, it isn't always the case.

Once again, you're the deciding factor. If you became pregnant the first time through ignorance, you shouldn't repeat the same mistake. You don't have to trap yourself in the cycle of continual pregnancy. Also, some women want many kids and enjoy having them. They should evaluate their ability to provide them with emotional, physical, and financial security.

Teen parents may have lots of strikes against them. Does that automatically mean you won't be good mothers and fathers? Some say you're too immature to handle the responsibility. Others feel you'll get bored and not care enough. You'll hold back your child's development. Still more believe that you don't have the necessary skills to offer the best for a child. There have been few studies on this subject, and most of these statements are hard to prove.

The teens I talked with were trying to be loving, attentive parents. At times it was hard, but parenting always is. Although in the beginning most of them didn't want to be pregnant, after the child was born they were happy with their decision not to have an abortion. When you have extra conflicts because of your age, these are reflected in how you treat and raise your child. There can be more difficulties than if you'd waited until you were more secure in all parts of your life. It is something you should remember. Can you provide the best home to an infant when you are still in your teens?

Sarah discussed her feelings on these interrelated issues as she mentally debated whether to have an abortion or have the baby. "The main advice I got," she said, "was to contrast the different potential outcomes. I feel I'm caught in the middle of what came first—the chicken or the egg. Does my pregnancy cause the problems or my problems cause the pregnancy? Is an abortion or unplanned baby harder to take physically and emotionally? Is it better to be a single parent or start a marriage as an expectant mother? It's too bad I can't settle for a chicken omelette and end all these questions."

Sarah's confusion is shared by the experts. They don't know for sure which are the causes and which the effects. Do teens quit school because of pregnancy and child rearing, or would they have stopped attending anyway? Are those the reasons for unemployment, or would they have had a hard time finding a job regardless? Do marriages among teens fail because of the couple's age, or because of lack of money, suitable work, etc.? The list could continue through each possible consequence of an early pregnancy.

Yes, there are obstacles, complications, problems, and challenges. Still you are all different. If you think hard, plan carefully, act wisely, you can prove the experts wrong and live a worthwhile, exciting, fulfilling life as a young parent.

CHAPTER 5
ABORTION–
ONE ALTERNATIVE

A pregnancy is a crisis—especially when it's unplanned and unwanted. In the Chinese language the
word for crisis contains two symbols written together.
One means "danger," the other "opportunity." Both
are possible in an unintended pregnancy. Yearly more
than 300,000 teens receive abortions, one alternative
to this unexpected event.

Before January 1973, abortions were generally
against the law. If you had money, you could risk your
life and obtain an illegal one. It might have been performed on a soiled kitchen table, in a motel, or the
back room of a deserted building. Under those conditions the procedure often proved highly dangerous.
Some women died. Others developed infections, became permanently sterile, or suffered from severe internal bleeding resulting from perforation of the

uterus. They couldn't complain, because they were breaking the law.

If you had both money and connections, you might have found a team of sympathetic doctors to certify that your emotional instability or physical well-being made an abortion necessary. Then you could have received one in a medical building, but you were made to feel very guilty. Some women traveled to Mexico, Sweden, or other countries that had more liberal abortion policies, but again this was an expensive proposition.

Although abortions are now legal, some doctors refuse to perform them. In certain places this service just doesn't exist. Add to that the fact that controversy continues to swirl around this option. On one side are those who say a woman has the right to have control over her body and should have the final word on whether or not she can provide a decent life for a possible child. They clash head-on with those who claim that aborting a fetus is murder. Lately there's been strong pressure to remove once more the choice of a legal abortion.

While polls prove that the majority of Americans believe we should allow women this alternative, the catch is back. For several years the federal government Medicaid program paid the bill if you couldn't afford an abortion. That's no longer true. Now only under special circumstances, such as when you're a rape victim and become pregnant as a result, will the government provide the money. Less than a handful of states are continuing to fund abortions for women who can't afford them, and daily the number decreases. So we've backtracked to, "Yes, you can have an abortion IF you have the money." And the majority of teenagers, most of whom previously received them for "free" because of Medicaid funding, can't come up with the money.

When abortions were illegal, those without money or influence sometimes tried to perform one themselves out of desperation. This may start happening again. Don't do it. Coat hangers, castor oil, swallowing pills, bumping down a flight of stairs, pounding yourself on the stomach won't work and can be lethal. These attempts just aren't worth it. Anything that's potent enough to abort a fetus will probably kill you as well.

If you decide that an abortion is the best solution, this is what you should do. The agency where you received your pregnancy test may have facilities for performing abortions. If you can't obtain the procedure there ask your counselor where to go. It might be a Planned Parenthood office, a local hospital, a health center, or an abortion clinic.

Wherever you decide to go, do it as soon as possible. Complications happen more often the further along you are in your pregnancy. Also, the cost is higher when you delay. The charge ranges from nothing, for those who might still qualify for Medicaid-funded abortions, up to about $500.

About half of the states require written, notarized, parental permission, or a parent present in the case of abortions for unmarried women under the age of eighteen. While this is being challenged in the courts, you should find out what the laws are in your community.

What can you expect when you go for your appointment? Although the process varies, these are the basic steps you'll follow. Beforehand you'll receive instructions on what to bring with you and how long the procedure will take. A counselor will meet you on the day of the event, explain the entire procedure, and answer any of your questions. Sometimes this is done individually. At other times a few women who will be receiving abortions talk together with an adviser.

You'll go to a laboratory where a technologist takes a small blood sample. This determines several things. Are you anemic? What is your blood type? Do you have a venereal disease? Often you'll provide another urine specimen to make sure you're pregnant. It will also be tested to see if your sugar and protein levels are normal.

Next a nurse accompanies you to an examining room where you put on a hospital gown. Your blood pressure, temperature, and pulse are taken. A doctor or nurse will ask you questions about your medical history. They want to find out if you are allergic to any drugs, have problems with blood clotting, and so forth. The physician will do an internal examination of your pelvic area to estimate how many weeks you are pregnant, as well as to figure out the position of your uterus.

If you have been pregnant for twelve weeks or less you are given a choice of a general or local anesthesia. When you choose a "general," you are put to sleep just before the procedure. Within ten seconds the anesthetic takes effect. During the recovery period, which usually lasts about an hour, you may feel nauseous, or a little dizzy. Some individuals briefly experience double vision. Another possible side-effect is cramps because your uterus is beginning to return to its normal size.

If you decide to have a local anesthetic, you'll be awake for the process. You're given Valium or sodium pentothal with a muscle relaxant. There might be a pinching sensation around the tip of your uterus. Then it becomes numb, so you have little if any pain. The recovery period is shorter—only about half an hour. Again, you may have cramps.

Lureen, seventeen, and many of her friends have had abortions. She offers this information and advice. "Since I've had two abortions, and gone with friends for theirs, let me tell you what to expect. When you know ahead of time, it's better. First you go to a health clinic. You talk to a counselor and learn anything special you have to know—like you're not supposed to eat for a few hours before you have it because it might make you sick. Don't worry. You won't starve.

"The clinic sets up an appointment for you. I think you should bring someone with you, so you don't feel alone. I'm going to tell you the truth. It does hurt a little. Don't listen to anybody that says it doesn't. If you believe them and it hurts just a bit, then you're going to exaggerate that pain. You shouldn't be scared, so it ends up hurting more than it should.

"To settle you down, they usually give you a Valium. Some of my friends want to be knocked out completely. That's up to you. I just wanted to get in and out of there as fast as possible. It's *not* a big, major operation. It's over before you know it."

There are different types of abortions. One technique is vacuum aspiration. This is used up to about the twelfth week of pregnancy. The physician very gently stretches open the cervix inside your vagina and then "vacuums" the interior of the uterine cavity. That's how the fetal tissue is removed. Afterward the doctor carefully scrapes the walls of the uterus to make sure all the tissue is gone. This whole procedure only lasts from six to ten minutes. Afterward you are brought into the recovery room.

Again, they take your blood pressure and pulse. If you're in pain, you are given medication to stop it. Sometimes you get tea, cookies, or crackers to munch on while you are recuperating. There is always a trained professional person nearby to help you in any way. Usually you're ready to go home within a few hours.

Counselors are available to give you birth control information and devices, and to schedule a follow-up appointment. Two to three weeks later you should have a final exam. This is for your own good, because you want to guarantee that there are no complications.

When you're more than twelve weeks pregnant, the procedure is different. You have either the dilatation and evacuation (D & E) or the instillation method. The doctor tells you which type will be used, based on your menstrual history, a pelvic examination, etc. These methods require you to stay in the hospital longer, so you may want to bring a bathrobe, slippers, and other personal items.

If you have a D & E, the cervix is temporarily dilated—made wider—and then the fetal tissue is taken out. With the instillation method, the physician injects a solution into your uterus to cause a miscarriage. This takes a few minutes and makes you feel a small amount of discomfort. They numb the area of injection to lessen the pain. The solution makes the uterus contract which *can* hurt. Then, within twelve to fourteen hours, a miscarriage occurs.

Usually you're admitted to the hospital early in the morning. You receive the medication around noon and miscarry during the evening or night. Then you can go home the next day. Sometimes it takes a little longer and you might have to stay in the hospital an extra day.

Before leaving you'll again talk with a nurse or counselor who will give you any instructions you might need and schedule a follow-up appointment. No matter which kind of abortion you receive, you should take it easy for a few days afterward. Generally there will be some bleeding that's similar to having a heavy menstrual period. Take care of yourself and do what the health people suggest.

There has been some research on teens' psychological reactions to having abortions. None evaluates how their male partners feel. I asked teens what emotions they experienced. Nearly all said relief was number one on their list. Others described themselves as feeling contented, proud they'd made a firm decision, free of moral conflicts about obtaining an abortion, and so on. A small number, about 15%, felt a little guilt or unhappiness. The few who had serious emotional problems usually had previous personal difficulties or had physical complications caused by the abortion.

It's been two years since Cindy had an abortion. When asked about her reactions she replied, "Emotionally it still hurts, but I think definitely in the long run it was the best thing for me to do."

Danielle expressed these thoughts. "I felt a lot of relief that it was over. I wasn't particularly depressed. Other friends of mine had gone through abortions, so it was pretty accepted among the group that I hung out with. There wasn't any feeling of having done something wrong. I never thought of it as killing a person."

For Penny the main term she used was "strange."

She elaborated, "While I was pregnant it was like it was somebody else's life. For about a month I wasn't living it. I'd stepped out of my body and was watching another person in a movie. Before I was petrified that I'd see one of my parents on the way to the clinic. Afterward I was just so glad it was over and I could get back to normal."

Caroline's main troubles were externally caused. She had to walk through a group of Right-to-Life members who were picketing outside of the health clinic. She explained, "I was emotionally vulnerable. They were screaming at me, 'You're a child murderer!' That made me feel awful, and then angry. They were taking advantage of me and the others at a point of low morale.

"I felt stupid for having gotten pregnant, but it would have been totally selfish for me to try and raise a child, because I was only fifteen. Now, a year later, I still feel no remorse. I'm really thankful I did make the decision to have an abortion. Occasionally I'll try to think of myself as a single parent and mentally imagine myself in that position. I have two sisters who are both single parents now. Even though they have jobs, family around, and a lot of support, it's really hard on them. It's turned their lives upside down. I'm glad I'm not them."

Bad emotional effects are most often minimized when you have people who care around you. Young women who had emotional support were least likely to be upset by the entire process.

Studies have been conducted to compare women who have abortions with those that carry the fetus full term. A summary of the findings reveals these characteristics for the ones who select the option of abortion: They are apt to be single and to use contraceptives. They also value control and exercise decision-making abilities over their lives; view themselves as strong, competent people; have a positive sense of self-worth; have high educational and/or employment aspirations; come from middle class or higher economic backgrounds. (This last factor could be explained by the cost of abortions. Poorer women may not be able to afford abortions, even though they want them.)

Deciding what to do about an unplanned pregnancy isn't easy. While you can ask others for advice, you should make the final choice. Joyce provided this information on how she finally arrived at her answer. A counselor provided the key. Joyce recalled, "When I was with the counselor I started to cry. I hardly ever do that. She said it wasn't worth having an abortion if that was going to ruin my life, *too*. I hadn't thought of it that way. She was good because she was objective. That really solidified it in my mind. I knew an abortion was going to hurt me real bad, but I didn't think it could ruin my life as much as having a child."

There are many more reasons why 300,000 teens ultimately select abortion as their solution. Those I interviewed frequently said they weren't ready for the responsibility. They were incapable of supporting a child either emotionally or financially. Often they talked of future plans and dreams. These would be very difficult or impossible to attain if their lives included a baby.

Patty Sue's father and brothers are ministers. She was very involved with church work when she learned she was pregnant. "I was real clear about what I wanted to do. There was never any question about not having an abortion. The only thoughts I have every now and then are around the date when the child would have been born. But I'm very glad I had the abortion.

"I have a good job and probably wouldn't have if I'd become a parent. The whole procedure was a very powerful experience in terms of my growth and how I thought of myself. I came out of it feeling real strong and being much surer about the kinds of relationships I wanted. For me a lot of it had to do with a good support system—my family and friends. It would have been absolutely unfair of me to bring another being into this world when I couldn't even take care of myself."

Most couldn't point to one reason; rather it came from a combination of circumstances. Some said they obtained an abortion primarily to keep the pregnancy a secret from as many people as possible. Jacqueline discussed her decision. "I was seventeen and just starting my whole life," she explained. "I didn't have any money, but I knew I could get Medicaid through the state to have an abortion. There were no moralistic qualms for me. I wasn't raised in any kind of religious background. If I had carried the child and either given it up for adoption or raised it, my parents would have known about it. And I didn't want them to find out. I didn't want to have to deal with any of their questions, anger, or dismay."

Having an abortion does not mean you can never have a child. Many teens, including Lureen, felt this fact influenced their decision. She said, "I knew I wasn't ready for an infant. Love can't buy things, pay the rent. Allen and I can always have a baby some other time. If we really love each other, we're going to be together for a while. I don't think of abortion as a 'method of birth control.' I didn't look forward to having one either, but I'm glad they're around. My final word of advice is the only sin with sex is unwanted pregnancy. That's my theory."

CHAPTER 6
CHECKLIST FOR EXPECTANT PARENTS

Each year 600,000 teenagers give birth rather than having an abortion or miscarrying. If you're one of those individuals, there are immediate plans to be made. After receiving confirmation of your pregnancy, you should begin prenatal—before the birth—care. It's vital to do this because without continual medical supervision your chances of having an easy nine months and a healthy baby decrease.

From the beginning of your pregnancy, you should be seeing a doctor, nurse, or midwife on a regular basis. That person oversees your progress about once a month until the twenty-eighth week. Then you get together every two weeks until the thirty-sixth week, and weekly after that.

During your visits you have your physical condition checked. You learn whether your pregnancy is going along all right. If the physician suspects there may be difficulties, he or she tries to remedy them. You should meet the doctor who will deliver your baby both to establish confidence and trust, and to eliminate any concerns you may have.

Good nutrition is always important, but even more so when you're pregnant. You could be eligible for the Special Supplemental Food Program for Women, Infants, and Children (WIC). It's sponsored by the U.S. Department of Agriculture and state health departments. They provide extra food for low-income pregnant and nursing women, their babies, and children under five. While there are WIC programs in all fifty states, Puerto Rico and the Virgin Islands, not all communities offer this service. To find out all the facts, phone the local branches of those departments.

As your pregnancy continues, it's natural to have questions. That's why you should either ask a health professional during your prenatal visits or seriously consider participating in childbirth preparation classes. These are conducted at hospitals, maternity homes, clinics, women's health centers, and other similar locations. More and more communities from large cities such as New York to smaller ones like Jackson, Mississippi; La Crosse, Wisconsin; and Oakland, California, have special programs geared just for expectant teen parents. These are tailored to your needs, so you don't feel like a Martian that fell from outer space.

The information covered includes everything from what physical changes you're experiencing, their causes and effects, advice on your diet, exercises, an explanation of the development of the fetus, through details about the new baby's needs. Paula said she resembled a human question mark until she started attending an adolescent maternity health clinic. She told why she goes. "I was convinced I was the *only* pregnant fifteen–year–old in the world. It really makes me feel better to be with girls my own age. We're all going through the same number together. Every Wednesday at the clinic a nurse sees me and doesn't make me feel stupid. Lots of times she brings up things I haven't even been able to ask.

"My body's making funny noises. My moods go up and down like they're cruising on an elevator. I thought I was coming unglued. My nurse told me little backaches, cramps, heartburn, that sort of stuff, doesn't mean I'm going to drop dead any second. They happen sometimes, 'cause you're pregnant. The veins in my legs started showing more and hurting. She said it's called 'varicose veins' and isn't all that unusual.

"My first three months I just about inhaled food. One hundred fifteen to one hundred fifty-six pounds before I realized elephants might want me to join up with them. My nurse helped me get on the right diet and learn how much weight gain is okay. Milk makes me sick, but I've been munching fruit, carrots, healthy things.

"Since I was dragging all the time, she explained how to rest, relax, and sleep properly. My friends thought it was a riot I had to learn how to kick back and take it easy. She kept saying smoking wasn't a good idea. I didn't stop, but I cut down. In the beginning I hid things from her, but then I confessed I was drinking some. She said I shouldn't, 'cause studies show it might damage my baby.

"This talking isn't at all like school. Everything has real meaning to me. I learn new words, too. I saw pictures of what the fetus is up to inside my body. My nurse is teaching me breathing exercises to practice, so labor won't hurt much. I heard about danger signs to warn me if something is getting funky. Last week my hands swelled up like balloons and she told me why and what to do.

"Since I'm almost due, we went on a tour of the delivery area. There was a film on childbirth. All this makes me not be afraid. These last couple of weeks we're talking mostly about what to do right after the baby's born. I don't think I would've done very good on my own. Now I'm ready for the hard part—being a momma."

Paula's program is typical. You also learn how to take care of your infant and hints of what to expect in the years to come. Knowing the best way to raise children doesn't come naturally. If it did, you might not have any problems with your parents. You discover the intricacies of your baby moving from milk and formula to solid foods, diaper changing, and what to do if your child becomes ill. And that's just the beginning. It's absolutely okay to have questions and receive answers. When you think you know everything is when you should worry.

Rochester, New York, is one of the leaders in the field of programs for expectant teen parents. Community members realized that the male partner needs attention, too. Though the majority of their services are designed for the mothers, boyfriends and husbands are included as well.

Ken and Carole didn't want marriage quite yet, but they're very important to each other. When Carole began attending the Rochester Adolescent Maternity Project, Ken decided to stop by and see what was happening. He said, "Carole started talking about 'prepartum care,' 'fetal development,' 'labor,' 'Caesarians.' It was like she was speaking a foreign language. Because I didn't know anything, I felt like a jerk.

"Finally I went to a group session they have for guys. For the first time I didn't feel like an outsider. We talked about our role, how we can help. Once one dude broke the ice and asked a question, it turned out we all needed advice. Having a kid isn't just a woman's thing. It has to do with making a family."

Young fathers participate more directly in the Bellevue, Washington, School Age Parent Program. You, as well as mothers, receive information on everything from details about the Maternal and Infant Health Program, to discussions on child abuse, community resources, students' rights, and contraception. You can even take cooking lessons. One father had an eleven–month–old daughter when he entered the program and eventually got married. A seventeen–year–old male attended for the school year, took the child growth and development class, but finally gave up his child for adoption.

In 1976 Dr. Helen M. Wallace, chairperson of the Maternal and Child Health Program at the University of California-Berkeley, helped survey nationwide services for pregnant teenagers in cities with populations of 100,000 and over. Less than one quarter of them provide any special work with the men. Towns smaller than 100,000 are the least likely to have any programs for adolescent females, let alone young men.

Prenatal care, childbirth preparation classes, and, of course, the actual hospital delivery, cost money. A few of you might be covered by insurance. Some of the childbirth classes are free. When you can't cover expenses, you should call your department of social services or a similar agency. It's definitely worth the effort, because you probably qualify for Medicaid. Remember that's a type of free health care provided by the government for people who can't afford to pay.

Terry agreed Medicaid made the difference for her. Without it, she might not have seen the inside of a medical facility until the day of delivery. She recalled,

"I was only sixteen when I got pregnant. Mom had some insurance through her job, but it didn't include anything like unwed pregnant daughters. I'd put her in a bad spot, so I felt I wanted to handle as much of the extra problems as I could. I got on the phone and started calling around. I talked to three different people before I finally got the right one and an appointment.

"At the Medicaid office, someone explained the basic steps for those that'd never applied before. Then I saw my assigned worker. I had to fill out forms, but he helped me and it didn't take that long. Even though I lived at home, I still qualified. My worker said if they could help me now, then my baby and I would be better-off in the long run. If I didn't have proper medical care, then it might cost everybody more later."

You've got the prenatal care and childbirth preparation under control. Money for medical expenses is temporarily covered. You're taking care of your body and your emotions. What happens if you want to keep exercising your mind and stay in school? Too often expectant teen mothers put this last on their list of things to do. It's hard to combine going to classes, getting ready for a new baby, and living in a body that's physically and emotionally zooming through roller-coaster changes. But the more formal education you have, the better are your chances for a secure, financial future for you and any little ones.

It took decades for everyone to accept the fact that academic attainment benefits pregnant adolescents. Formerly the minute school administrators found out you were pregnant, you were forced to quit. They acted as if they thought pregnancy was contagious. Other students would catch your "disease" if you remained in the classroom. You represented a "bad influence" on your peers.

Then in 1972 our government banned sex discrimination in educational facilities receiving federal aid. To guarantee that the point is clear, and expectant mothers won't be expelled, new regulations were issued to Title IX in 1975 that specifically deal with pregnancy.

Now the choice is yours. Because community policies differ, you should contact your board of education or talk to your counselor for details. Some school systems provide home tutors. In other locations you keep going to your same school. Occasionally teachers and students will treat you as if you're in the last stages of leprosy. You know you aren't and shouldn't let them make you feel uncomfortable. Other areas have advanced further. They have separate programs that combine normal course work with instruction similar to childbirth preparation and parenting classes.

Luella participates in one of San Francisco's six Special Service Centers located in a hospital. She's able to continue her education and also has many people on hand to assist her overcome any difficulties. There are nutritionists, health educators, teachers, nurses, occupational therapists, doctors, and equally important—new friends.

Without the center, Luella said, "I would've been up a creek. Whenever I felt down, there was someone around to help me smile. The center has a little nursery, so I've been getting practice being a mother. At first I was going to quit school, but this place is different. I've learned how necessary a diploma is to my future and my baby's. I don't want to be on welfare all my life and now maybe I won't."

There are similar programs in such diverse cities as New York; Pittsburgh, Pennsylvania; Atlanta, Georgia; Evanston, Illinois; Oklahoma City, Oklahoma, and Westminster, Colorado. The New Futures School in Albuquerque, New Mexico, is one of the very best and most comprehensive. Because of this, Caroline Gaston, the director, was requested to testify before the U.S. Senate Human Resources Committee in June 1978. She began by describing their students.

"At New Futures School, 47% of the girls are Spanish surnamed, 35% are Anglo (white), 8% are Black, and 8% are Native American Indians. The average age is sixteen. Our youngest girls have been twelve years old, in the sixth grade. Some programs see even younger girls. Most (75%) are single. A sizable number have had previous pregnancies, many terminated by abortions. Nearly a third were school dropouts prior to the pregnancy. Half of them read at or below sixth grade reading level." As with the Special Service Centers in San Francisco, there are a wide range of professionals to offer support, understanding, and technical assistance.

Gaston discussed a representative student named Teresa. She was two months pregnant when she quit school, four months along when she entered New Futures.

One counselor told Teresa about the classes from which she might choose—typical subjects like English, history, math, and physical education. Family Living is required. In that course she learns "that good parenting begins with prenatal attitudes and habits." The other requirement is Child Development. Expectant mothers have experience with kids under the direction of nursery helpers and child development specialists.

A nurse interviewed Teresa to obtain her health history. Although she hadn't seen a doctor even for a pregnancy test, she knew the symptoms from an earlier one that ended with an abortion. After that first consultation, Teresa received regular medical attention from the Maternity and Infant Care Program. She became depressed, but with weekly group counseling and individual sessions she began feeling "better about herself and more positive about her future."

New Futures School tries to consider the broader picture of a teen pregnancy. The impact on the family, young father, and career plans aren't overlooked. Gaston continued, "Teresa's mother took part in the counseling group for parents. . . . Teresa's boyfriend, who had told her during the time they were dating that he would stand by her 'if anything should happen,' had stopped seeing her soon after he learned of her pregnancy. This happens with many of the girls, but there are some young fathers, both married and unmarried, who participate in evening couples' counseling groups."

After Teresa gave birth to a healthy baby girl, a nurse visited her at home to make sure everything was all right. Two weeks after the delivery, Teresa returned to finish the semester and brought her baby to the school nursery. When her daily enrollment ended, she joined a follow-up group.

She graduated from high school, has a full-time job and "is able to afford to place her child in day care. Teresa's problems have not all been solved, but we believe she is well on her way to becoming a contributing member of our community."

As you can see, taking care of yourself during pregnancy involves time, thought, and work. This is just as true of planning for after the baby's arrival. In those intervening months you'll feel countless emotions. All young, expectant mothers learn there are benefits and disadvantages to being pregnant.

Prior to becoming pregnant teens often have no

direction. Nothing in their lives seems very important. With the news of impending parenthood, they realize they have a specific purpose. They have a greater meaning for themselves, as well as a child to plan for. No longer do they drift from activity to activity. They have serious decisions to make, appointments to keep, and plans for the future.

Many thoroughly enjoy the experience of pregnancy. They detail their fun, wonderment, and anticipation. Another being is growing inside them. They are intrigued and fascinated by all the changes they notice. Often their positive reactions are reinforced by the love they receive from special people in their lives.

Phyllis, sixteen, delighted in her pregnancy. She explained further, "For once I felt important. I wasn't just thinking of me. I was amazed by all the changes. The first time the baby kicked, I put my hand on my stomach and felt such excitement and pride. I'd created another person. What could be more significant than that? I wanted to work and succeed even more because now it was for two of us—not only me."

Kimberly, twenty-one, describes her marital status as "zero." From thirteen to sixteen she'd gone steady and hadn't become pregnant. After she and her boyfriend broke up, she had a summer romance with Bill. By September she was pregnant, but she waited three months until she had a urine test to confirm it. For "emotional reasons" she decided against abortion. After her first dismay, she soon looked forward to the birth. Her whole face lit up when she talked about her pregnancy.

"I *loved* it. It was nice, easy, and seemed really short. Since I'd blocked the first part, I felt like I was only pregnant for four months. What made the entire difference for me was the atmosphere here in my family and with my friends. I didn't mind knowing my baby would be illegitimate, because it didn't bother anybody else. Even now I never pretend I've been married the way some girls do."

The years Pat and her husband, Craig, have spent together have been a realistic picnic—enough ants to cause irritation, but sufficient happiness to make it worthwhile. When she became pregnant the second time at sixteen, she quit school and took the high school equivalency exam (GED). After a lot of discussion Pat and Craig decided to get married. Another decision was that she wanted to have natural child birth using the Lamaze method. Craig went along to the classes, so they both felt prepared for the delivery.

"I'd like to be pregnant the rest of my life," Pat smiled. "I felt so calm and serene, so at peace with myself. Although I've always been a very nervous person, during my pregnancy I was completely relaxed. I was in good health. I never felt better. It was marvelous. Craig was really wonderful to me. He never even complained near the end of my pregnancy, when we couldn't have sex any more."

When adolescents had difficulties they were often caused by other peoples' reactions to their pregnancy. Joan said she was pleased being pregnant. While she didn't have any physical problems, she did have to deal with emotional ones. She said, "When I was four months pregnant, the father and I were going to get married, but then he freaked out. He was really scared. We'd been living together for a few months and I had to move out. My parents let me return home and they took care of me. So from about three months to six months along I was upset the whole time. Then I settled down and enjoyed the rest of it."

A pregnancy can produce some negative responses. Many expectant adolescents talked about a sense of alienation or isolation from their family and friends. While others might not have intended to leave them out of activities, this sometimes happened. Because they have new concerns besides dating, grades, and parties, they sometimes felt alone and excluded.

Cathleen stated, "The pregnancy wasn't too bad until I got to be about six months. Then I started to feel really different, apart from all my friends that weren't pregnant. That meant 99% of them. I kind of felt like an old lady. My husband, Tony, and I seemed just so in-between. When you're pregnant the responsibility starts to change you. We didn't fit in with other couples that'd been married for a while or with my school friends. It really puts you in a spot.

"Tony'd get mad at me. 'All you ever want to do is stay home,' he'd say. I couldn't drink, do drugs, or even smoke cigarettes, without getting sick to my stomach. That put me in a different place, too. Not being able to have fun with all my friends. Then Tony started going out by himself and leaving me at home. I'd go into hysterics. I just felt really lonely, but it's hard for me to talk about my feelings. I keep everything bottled up inside. I'd cry myself to sleep worrying about the fix I'd gotten into and especially that the baby might not come out right.

"Things did start picking up near the end of my pregnancy. People would come over with presents. I'd been really bored with my life before all this started happening, so I was ready for something different. I've got to laugh, getting pregnant and married, now that was a change!"

Other disadvantages to being pregnant stem from factors that are indirectly related. Your future will be radically changed. Decisions are necessary. It's normal for expectant mothers to be concerned about the health and welfare of the new baby. Occasionally all these various issues seem overwhelming. They are too much to handle and emotional troubles surface. This is more likely to happen when you've had problems before the pregnancy. That new situation heightens previous ones.

Andrea, seventeen, expressed it this way. "I'd never had to think about more than myself. Before the pregnancy a major decision for me was what to wear to school. All of a sudden I was supposed to act like an adult even though I knew I was still a kid."

Another seventeen–year–old, Nancy, also had difficulties. She comes from an upper middle class family. Because her grades were superior, her parents believed everything was fine. They weren't. She was pregnant, scared, and very depressed. "I admit I had a lot of problems, but many started before I got pregnant. I dropped out of school and stayed home most of the time. The day of the homecoming game, I stayed in bed and cried.

"For a while I got on a real self-destruct trip. I wasn't eating right and felt blah. The doctor said I was suffering from anemia. If I wanted a healthy baby, I'd have to take better care of myself. He was worried because I hadn't seen a doctor until I was five and a half months along. I even thought about suicide. I took a couple of downers, but not enough to really do the job. My pregnancy wasn't fun."

Nancy is in the small minority. After the initial shock wears off, more adolescent expectant mothers offer glowing accounts of this time of their lives. While there are moments when they feel "fat and ugly," these quickly subside. Many people believe that women are most beautiful when they are pregnant. Without bragging, the teens I interviewed agreed. They'd never felt as lovely as during those months.

CHAPTER 7
SINGLE AND PREGNANT? SPECIAL NEEDS, SPECIAL SOLUTIONS

Single and pregnant? Expectant mothers in this category sometimes have special needs that require special solutions. Maybe you want to live away from your home during your pregnancy. Until as recently as fifteen or twenty years ago, the main reason a woman did this was to keep "her condition" a secret. She was packed off to a residential maternity home in another community. Meanwhile her family concealed the truth with weird explanations that their daughter was visiting relatives in Timbuktu, or attending a boarding school in Iceland.

Although a number of these homes have closed, others have adjusted to current times and remain open with expanded programs. Generally they're run by the Salvation Army, the Florence Crittenton League, or certain religious organizations. Teens often turn to these places now because they have extra difficulties. A Florence Crittenton executive in a metropolitan area describes a "typical" resident as "single . . . usually between fifteen and seventeen years of age—on welfare—a court ward—from a nearby area. (She) is usually physically and emotionally neglected. . . . She must be taught how to love without having known love, or how to share with others. She has only survived by fighting for everything she is."

While the services vary, those that the Crittenton agencies provide are representative. They have individual and group counseling designed to help you with any emotional and family relationship problems, as well as with your decisions about the pregnancy and plans for the child. You have medical and health care —prenatal, delivery, family planning, child care, nutrition, etc. Your academic and vocational education is covered, even including job counseling. You get guidance on finances, future housing, and appropriate community resources. You can make arrangements for legal advice on your rights and those of your child. There are recreational and cultural activities. Finally, most have some kind of program for the fathers and the grandparents.

There are homes in Mobile, Alabama; Phoenix, Arizona; Little Rock, Arkansas; Los Angeles, California; Denver, Colorado; Savannah, Georgia; Sioux City, Iowa; Topeka, Kansas; Boston, Massachusetts; Detroit, Michigan; Helena, Montana; Columbus, Ohio; Nashville, Tennessee; Wheeling, West Virginia; and other cities. For more information you should check your telephone directory under Salvation Army, Florence Crittenton, or call your department of social services. Within these homes you'll find love, support, understanding, and sound advice.

Joanne was nervous when she first moved into the Salvation Army White Shield Home in Portland, Oregon.

For the last eight years she'd been with a series of foster families. At sixteen she was skeptical of social workers and tired of what she called "do-gooders." Her opinion softened after she spent ten months in this maternity home.

"I felt like a number when I walked through the door," Joanne stated. "I'd been bounced from place to place, seen so many counselors and therapists that I treated it like a game. I thought the same thing would happen here. To make a long story short, they helped me pull my life together. Some of the other girls were just as bummed out as I was in the beginning. We learned how to help each other and ourselves. After I had my kid, I still was kind of shaky in my head. They let me stay on for six months until I felt stronger. I think I'm finally ready to start doing it on my own."

Many more of you might be interested in taking advantage of these services without living there. This is possible in most cases. Although you stay at your own home, you may participate in the programs that'll help you the most. Maybe you'll want suggestions on prenatal care or schooling. The staff members can either help you directly or recommend where you should go. You might not have made up your mind about whether you want to keep the child. They will refer you to the correct place to go for more information. Many agencies are developing follow-up programs, also. After your baby's birth, you won't be alone. You can look to them for counseling and further referrals. Some teens said they preferred living at home, but attending these programs during the day. This took away the disadvantage of missing their friends and family or being afraid when they were on their own.

Dawn returned to her family each night. She said

she liked the idea of having such complete help "under one roof." At the same time she felt better knowing that her mother was nearby. "I got the best of both situations," Dawn explained. "I was scared not to have familiar faces around. Still I wanted to be with girls my age. My mom couldn't do everything for me. I felt like I was taking charge of my life.

"The whole experience brought us closer together. I'd tell my mom what I'd learned. She was really surprised. Even though she'd had four kids, she didn't seem to know as much about what to eat, what help there was in the community, and things like that. I'd really recommend going to these programs, if there's one in your neighborhood."

Single and pregnant? What can you do if you realize you aren't quite ready for motherhood? For decades foster care has been a "temporary" solution. Either on a formal or informal basis, you make arrangements for someone else to look after your child for a while. When this is done formally, you work with your department of social services. While meeting with a staff member you learn everything you should know about the procedure. You find out about the family with whom your child will stay. You're told how often and when you may visit that home to keep up contact. And you're continually told about your baby's progress.

Informal foster care means that on your own you let a relative or friend temporarily take on the main responsibility for raising your infant. In both cases, formal or informal, legally the child remains yours. When you feel ready to make a final decision, it's your right to have your baby back. One of the major advantages of this is the breathing space—time to evaluate what's best for the two of you. Meanwhile you know the child will be fed, clothed, housed, and enjoyed by people who care. Simultaneously you're free to regain your strength, maybe find a job, continue school, and adjust to your changed life.

Even though this might sound great and can be, too often it isn't. What starts out to be a stopgap measure for a few weeks or months, frequently ends up as a permanent situation. While you waver in your decision, the months roll into years. That tiny baby drifts toward two years old, then six, and suddenly is a full-grown teenager.

During those years the child may be moved from foster family to foster family. Deborah Shapiro reported in her book *Agencies and Foster Children,* that foster care of no more than three or four years can be handled by children. They were "evaluated by their (social) workers as healthy, developing normally, and relatively free of major emotional disturbance." Beyond that period the arrangement becomes more complicated.

One Massachusetts study of 6,000 foster children painted a gloomier picture. It revealed that especially after as much as three years had passed, they were "often damaged kids, fearful of further trauma, lacking in self-worth, distrustful, angry, longing to love yet fearing to love." From one day to the next, they never knew how long they'd stay with their current foster parents.

This isn't nearly as confusing for the offspring when the mother informally agrees to have members of her (or the father's) family raise the child. That happens frequently, primarily among blacks and lower income groups. Grandparents, uncles, aunts, and cousins pitch in to blanket the new member of the family with love and security. The real mother is often right there, but she has a lot of help from others. The child doesn't grow up feeling abandoned to a series of strangers.

Giving up a child, even for a little while, can be an emotional event for a mother. I talked to teens who decided that foster care was necessary. How did they feel during the separation? Although there was no standard answer, often they remembered they were lightened of the immediate pressure but not as much as they thought they'd be. Sure, the pregnancy was over, but their problems weren't. They were merely putting them off while they searched for the best solution.

Some said the experience seemed "unnatural." They felt "funny," as if they didn't really have a child. Others told me they became very depressed and restless. They knew they should make decisions, but they didn't know where to start. Few of these reactions occurred when the baby remained within the young mother's home. When the infant was placed with strangers these strong emotions were more likely to happen. As time went by the teen mothers' feelings generally smoothed out. They were mentally more stable and better prepared to make serious choices.

Conflicts within themselves and with the foster parents do arise, but often they diminish rapidly. When Alicia was sixteen she gave birth to a baby boy. Before that she'd been into drugs, cutting classes, and some minor illegal activities. All that didn't mean she would be a poor parent. She said, "I knew I was a wreck when Jason was born. I'd blown a lot of things in my life and he seemed like a second chance. Also I realized I wasn't in any shape to start him off right. I'd tried for about a month and it just was making everything worse.

"After a big go 'round with my social worker, she suggested foster care. Jason would still have my last name. The worker would set it up so I could visit him when I wanted to. Because the family'd get money for watching him, I figured they'd do a good job. It seemed okay. That'd give me time by myself to find a place to live, save a little money, and get my head on straight. If I couldn't do it, then I'd have to think of something else for him.

"The first time I saw him with his foster mother, it was kind of creepy. He was crying when I came in and I thought, 'Oh no, she's a terrible person. I'm making a mistake leaving him there.' The foster mother and I talked some. I learned she'd had responsibility for different kids for almost five years. Once she had three at one time. She had two teenagers of her own. She told me, 'All babies cry. Since they can't talk, it's their way of communicating. It might mean they're hungry, want their diapers changed or just a little loving and attention.' That made me feel better.

"Now it's been almost seven months. Things aren't happening as fast as I thought they would. I haven't been seeing Jason as much as before. That makes me feel sort of guilty. I don't think about him all the time, the way I did in the beginning. I'm still not sure what's best. When I do see him I get a bit jealous of his foster mother. He doesn't even seem to know who I am. My worker doesn't push me too hard. We get together regularly to talk. Sometimes I wish somebody'd say, 'Alicia, you have to do this or that.' Making final decisions has always been rough for me."

Single and pregnant? Some adolescent mothers decide that placing their infant with an adoptive family is the answer for them. Since the legalization of abortion and the decrease in forcing single parents to rush out and get married, fewer people consider this option. It's still available and may be the best solution for you.

Because this procedure is different depending on where you live, you should talk with a social worker, doctor, minister, rabbi, priest, or lawyer to find out exactly what you must do. Basically this is what happens in a legal adoption process.

(1) You, the natural parent, give consent allowing the infant to be adopted.

(2) The couple (or single person) who wants to adopt the child completes the required application.

(3) The prospective parents are investigated and interviewed to make sure they're capable of providing the infant with an emotionally and financially stable home.

(4) There is a court hearing to guarantee the consent forms are in order and the adoptive parents have been approved. If this has been taken care of, the court issues an "interlocutory decree" that allows the child to be placed with the new parents.

(5) The baby remains with the adoptive parents for the waiting period that is required by law before the procedure becomes final. This is usually from six months to a year. Within that time the adoptive or natural parents can change their minds, but this happens infrequently and can be difficult for everyone concerned.

(6) The court issues a final decree stating the child is the legal responsibility of the adoptive parents and ending all your rights.

Once you decide on adoption, you'll be guided and advised through all these steps. There are good and bad points to this option. The teens I questioned said they were relieved to know their child would be in a warm, loving home being raised by caring people. That thought helped them face their own new lives with peace of mind. The most serious disadvantages they mentioned were the permanency of their decision and dealing with their conflicting emotions.

As with any emotional event, feelings are different depending on the person. Immediately after the birth of the child some of the teens went through reactions like those who gave their infants into temporary foster care away from their homes. But those placing their baby with an adoptive family sometimes had a more severe reaction because this situation is harder to reverse. In most cases you just aren't going to see your child again.

Many of the adolescents were confused and wondered whether they had done the right thing. Would the child be "okay?" What was the family like? What kind of future would the infant have? The teens described themselves as "aimless," "depressed," or having an overwhelming "sense of loss." They'd gone through an entire pregnancy, delivered a baby, and now there was nothing. They felt physically and emotionally empty. Some wanted to talk about all the thoughts going on in their minds. Others wanted to keep everything inside at least for a while. This intense grief, longing, and despair lasted from a few days to a few weeks.

Time does help solve problems and soothe painful memories. As the weeks lengthened into months their spirits improved. Most of them resumed their previous activities and turned to the future instead of worrying about the past. Unfortunately, they said, there was no way to predict when renewed depression might hit. Maybe they'd see kids at a playground and feel sad, guilty, or remorseful. Or a friend gave birth. It was their baby's birthday. Any of these events might or might not make them feel down.

Within six to ten weeks these heavy reactions weren't as bad. A few mentioned they'd become upset because they felt they should be MORE concerned. They couldn't remember what the baby looked like. Some of them criticized themselves. Maybe they were too conceited and self-centered. They should care more. Perhaps this meant they'd never be good parents.

At this period some started thinking about the infant's future again. They looked to other people for reassurance that they'd done the right thing. Was it normal to be feeling separate and distant from the child? All these situations and emotions eased up when special people—their own families, friends, boyfriends—let them know they still cared.

The majority of the teens agreed it helped a lot when key individuals like their social worker or counselor directly discussed certain commonly shared experiences. For example, during a pregnancy and the adoption procedure it's normal to be angry, despondent, isolated, and troubled. It's just as normal NOT to feel those emotions. This is a perplexing time, but you can and generally do mature as a result of it.

Placing a child with an adoptive family is a mature, selfless act. Ultimately you are thinking of the child's well-being. You are giving something *to* the child, not giving *away* the baby. When reminded of this, your dismay and guilt should decrease.

There are no absolute answers to such questions as: Is it better to see the child after the delivery? Should you briefly nurse and feed the baby before the adoption and separation takes place? How will you feel if your child later tries to find you? What do you want the adoptive parents to tell the child about you and your partner? Will you think a lot about the child as the years go by?

Charlotte regretted nursing her baby for a few days in the hospital. She believed it made the final separation worse. "I don't think I would have felt as lonely and empty if I'd never seen him. Now I have firm memories that are harder to erase."

Barbara was glad she spent a little time with her newborn. She said, "Finally curiosity entered in. I wanted to see her to make it real, because the whole period seemed unreal to me. That baby came out of me. I wanted to touch and hold her."

Kim was seventeen when she gave birth. She was willing to talk at length about many facets of this experience. How did she decide that adoption was best for her? How did she feel about seeing the baby? What was her opinion of her counselor? How does she feel now, several years later? Her words provide this overview.

"At first I considered keeping the baby. I'm not sure how or when I made my final decision. You can't zero in on a single item. One thing was visiting my sister, brother-in-law, and their new infant for a few weeks. They'd planned this, wanted a child, and were secure in their love. I came away realizing how little I had to offer by myself. I felt very guilty, because I thought it was a cover-up for my selfishness. Was it wrong for me to say, this is what's best for me? Then I knew I had to think what was really best for my child.

"In the back of my mind I believe I'd already chosen adoption, but I needed someone to convince me or give me permission that it was okay. All the times I went to the counselor, the only worthwhile thing she said was, 'You have to live with your choice. Don't listen to anybody, but yourself.'

"I talked to her about the advantages and disadvantages of seeing the child after she was born. She said I could, but at first the nurse was against the idea. She told me, 'It's been advised that you don't see her.' It was a real fight to let me do that. I had to clear up my mind. When I did manage to see her I was absolutely overwhelmed. I remember thinking, 'Gee, she's cute. She's got white hair like me when I was born.' Then I felt numb, depressed. There were so many emotions those first couple weeks I don't know what to call them all.

"Soon I felt very right about adoption for the baby, because watching her being born and touching her told me this child has a right to live and to live a good life. I have the right to make the same choice for myself—like a rebirthing for me.

"People tell me I've 'adjusted' so well to the adoption. What they mean is I've done something wrong. My belief is it's an okay process and you should adjust. It's all right not to feel guilty any more. It's all right not to spend every day worrying where the child is. It's almost like people think you're abnormal if you're normal about it.

"Another question I get is do I ever think about my child. My answer—very, very seldom. I'm sure my niece is a wee bit spoiled by me because she's about the same age as mine, but I feel very secure in my decision. I never sit and worry about how she's developing, if she's happy. I don't think of it as being intentional—like I've got to make sure I'm busy so I don't think about her. The first few weeks were hard, of course, but not now.

"I have no desire to track down my child. I won't go kidnap her. I'm curious, but not enough to search through records and hang around playgrounds looking for someone who resembles me. Plus I told the agency I didn't want her placed in the county where I live. We have our own lives to live—separately.

"One more standard question is do I have any fantasies about her seeking me out when she's older. I imagine I fantasize. It wouldn't bother me if she showed up on my doorstep. I think what does concern me more is this whole issue of kids hunting down their biological mother. And it's always her. It's never, 'I've got to find that guy.' If my daughter couldn't exist without finding me, would it mean I didn't make the right decision? When I went through the final part of the adoption with the lawyer, I gave them a lot of information about our backgrounds. Educational, health, family origins. My daughter has access to all that when and if she wants to know.

"This entire experience has made me stronger. I feel worthwhile and good about myself now, but it took a long time. Maybe that is my last message. Don't expect change to be something easy. It's very frightening, painful, and sometimes lonely. But you can do it."

CHAPTER 8
RAISING A CHILD

Mother. Father. Mom. Dad. Those are words that you reserved for your parents. Those people are adults. You love them. You hate them. They set rules for you. You follow them. You ignore them. You feel barriers and you feel closeness. Now suddenly you, too, are a parent.

What's it like being a parent? Can reading about other teens' experiences help prepare you for this drastic change in your life? If nothing else, maybe these next pages can give you some clues. Continually the adolescents I interviewed said they had no idea what to expect in their new role. They wished somewhere, somehow, they had gained a little insight beforehand. Any situation is easier when you have an outline of what might unfold. The expectant parents were nervous, fearful, and concerned, yet at the same time they were excited.

Most of them also agreed with Penny's comments. Because she had been a baby sitter, helped with her younger brother, she thought she knew enough about raising a child. Even if this weren't the case, she acknowledged, "Whatever people were telling me, I just wasn't ready to hear. I don't know if it's possible to learn from anybody else. Maybe our words will make a stronger impression, because we've been there. I think I would have paid more attention to a person my own age instead of all those adults. They seemed to lecture, not speak from similar situations and pressures. How could they really comprehend what I was going through without having been a kid trying to bring up a kid."

Rochelle, sixteen, has a three–month–old baby. She told me the first lesson she had to understand was "the only trouble with parents is you've never been one before. You'll make mistakes, but you'll also delight in your successes. You'll have good days, bad days, and some that are a combination of both."

Raising a child is rewarding, joyous, and meaningful. It's also time-consuming, demanding, and a huge responsibility. This is a commitment which is always present. A baby isn't a toy that you can put aside if the novelty wears off. Barbara is almost twenty. Three years ago she walked down the aisle four months pregnant. Her attitude is positive and realistic. She's dedicated to this theory. "You've got that child for the rest of your life. When you're eighty years old, you're still going to worry about him even if he's over sixty. And you should. You can't just say, 'Sorry kid. I'll see you later.' "

Al, a seventeen-year-old father, pointed out, "I never want to be average in anything I do. But in order to have the peaks—the highs—you've got to deal with the valleys—the bummers. My best and worst moments have come from this first year of fatherhood."

For parents, there are practical skills to master coupled with emotional reactions to confront. While this is true for any new parent, the challenge is frequently compounded for adolescents because of your age. Imagine the life of a typical teenager who is not a parent. Maybe it's not always great, but when it comes to responsibilities, decisions, and activities—you can think of yourself first. Now, as a parent, that's completely changed. If you thought you had sacrifices and hardships before, you haven't seen anything yet.

Babette mentioned that before her baby's birth she considered a heavy decision meant whether to order pizza or a hamburger. If she felt like cutting class, she would. She could sleep as long as she wanted to on the weekends. Her parents might battle about money, but that was their problem. Her home was comfortable. Her wardrobe adequate. There was always plenty of food on the table. Although she had certain duties around the house, she sometimes procrastinated. All this changed when she became a mother.

In the beginning babies are totally dependent on others for every need. Without help they can't sit up, talk, or eat. Someone has to dress them, bathe them, soothe and love them. And that's just the start of a parent's responsibilities. For the new mother those constant demands come when you haven't fully regained your physical strength after childbirth. Your hormones are returning to normal, while your emotions race up and down. Graciella has a month-old baby,

Maria. She wanted to discuss both the practical side of these last four weeks, and why she feels the sacrifices are worthwhile.

She explained, "Little babies don't sleep the way we do. Maria naps maybe three or four hours, wakes up and I breast feed her. That's just magic, holding her so close. After that I have to rest her against my shoulder and burp her.

"Next I've got to change her diapers. Then she gurgles or cries and falls asleep. A few hours later it's the same thing all over again. I usually give her a bath every day, too. I didn't know how to do any of this. Sometimes I space out, because I'm so tired. An infant just doesn't give you any *time* to rest yourself and recover. I don't think I've ever been so exhausted in my life. I started getting really down. Mom says it happens to every woman. They call it 'post partum blues,' and it happens shortly after the baby's birth. The change in my hormones causes it.

"You know with everything there's a balance. Maria is such a wonderful child. It's like there's a bond between us. She just loves me so much, more than anyone ever has. I get so turned on now that her eyes have started to focus. She looks straight at me, like she knows who I am. If I put my finger in front of her, she'll reach up with this tiny hand and make a fist around it. Yesterday she really smiled for the first time. If you've never been a mother it's hard to explain. That might not seem like a big deal, but it was so beautiful for me. I can hardly wait to see what she'll do next."

The practical side doesn't end there. You have to learn how to make formula, and how to remain calm when you discover that your little darling has set the house on fire. There are temper tantrums, crying spells, illnesses, and countless other events that are all part of growing up.

Time after time the young mothers and fathers stressed the loving and nurturing aspect of being a parent. Kimberly stated, "Everybody expects horror stories about being a teenage mother, but for me it's been great. And I'm saying that from my heart. It's been rough, sure, but the loving part's been more than I ever dreamed."

The list of benefits is endless. The interviewees talked about the thrill of watching and helping another being develop into a self-sufficient person. Each day was a new adventure. As they participated in this process, they realized that they in turn were growing and maturing. They sensed a stronger independence within themselves. They became more fulfilled than ever before.

At seventeen, Cathy gave birth to her first child. Now, three years later and the mother of two, she expressed these feelings. "We're growing up together. As my kids' abilities increase, so do mine. I do feel a lot older than other girls my age, but that's because I have a more serious purpose in life."

In honesty the teen parents brought up the disadvantages. The total responsibility could swell into a burden. Spontaneity was no longer possible. Their lives were restricted because they had to think of their child. Kimberly continued, "My life came to a screeching halt when I got pregnant and had Brandy. It's an enormous amount of responsibility that no seventeen-year-old should have. Especially when they're babies, it's trying. You've got to be strong yourself and surrounded by strong and helpful people if you're going to get through it.

"Even though it's three years later, the responsibility's there. It never quits. It just comes in different stages. Now I have to talk to her all the time. Tell her stories. Try to teach her things. There's none of this let's watch TV all day. I catch myself sometimes and think I'm being so damn lazy. I say, 'Brandy, go get a book.' Boom, she runs off to find one. I think I've been ignoring this poor kid for hours. She hasn't been bugging me at all. She's such a sweetheart and always has been. Now she's at the point where she's getting her own will. She says things that make me cry they're so funny, but all this is a lot of work. I'm tied down and can't do a lot of things."

Kimberly wasn't the only one to mention this aspect. Suddenly a whole new set of priorities had to be established. Cathleen described how this affected her. "At times I feel like I've missed things that others my age are doing. I can't be free, not now or even for the next years and years. I have the responsibility for another human being. When someone asks me to do something, first I have to think if I can afford the money. If I can, I have to find a baby sitter—more money. By then sometimes I don't even want to go out, because it's such a hassle."

Lilly said she could no longer be selfish. She had to think of more than just herself and her pleasure. Because she is young, occasionally she tries too hard to be a "super mother." She wants to do everything exactly right. When the baby wouldn't stop crying, Lilly "broke down and yelled at him." She felt both guilty about her reaction and resentful toward him. This child was intruding on her privacy and life. Then within seconds her anger at herself would intensify. How could she blame her baby? He hadn't asked to be brought into the world. She had done that. Now she has to offer him the best home, devotion, and care of which she is capable.

For all young parents other potential trouble spots include conflicts in child-raising techniques, money, and finding day care facilities. Single parents were more likely than married couples to bring up disagreements with their own mothers and fathers on how best to handle the infant. While they welcomed help and advice, the teens are convinced they have to establish their independence.

For financial reasons many single parents initially return home after the baby's birth. This eases some of their fears of inadequacy and inexperience, but it does create a different problem. Their parents still treat them as "children" and feel they know best. Betty elaborated on this issue. "My mother and I had a series of arguments about who had the final word in raising Holly. I'd say to my mom, 'Look, would you let me raise her, please. You're in my way.'

"She'd come back, 'You don't appreciate me.'

"I'd counter, 'Yes, I do, but just let me take over. I can do it.' "

Many adolescent parents were glad to have the responsibility shared with their family. It was a backup they needed until they felt better able to cope with their role. Often this experience made them become closer to their own parents. Almost as equals they could discuss what thoughts and emotions they were having. They were reassured when their mothers and fathers would reminisce about those very same confused moments.

Antonia, fifteen, is convinced she couldn't have gotten through her first year without her parents' support. She felt young, vulnerable, frightened and alone. Although her mother tried to alleviate these concerns, at night Antonia had the greatest pressure. "During the day I was fine. Then came the night and everyone went to sleep—except Jonathan. I looked at him and started to cuss him out. Then I thought, 'What am I doing?' Here was this baby and I didn't even feel close to him. He was yelling his head off and I wanted to sleep.

"I thought it was a natural instinct to love your baby from the minute the infant's born. I was petrified to be by myself with him. I wanted to be warm to him. I'd pick him up and try to do the right thing. But when he'd keep crying, I'd get mad. There was always something that had to be done. I never seemed to have time for myself.

"Finally I broke down and opened up to my mother. She said I had lots of reasons to be upset. It was okay that I didn't feel love right away. Some parents do, but with others they have to work through their own problems before they can give of themselves to another. Together we sat down and wrote out a schedule. Now things have eased up. I'm proud of myself, Jonathan, and my mother for being there when I needed her most."

The majority of single teen mothers qualify for Aid to Families with Dependent Children (AFDC). This federal government program may reduce some of your money fears. Each month a check is paid to the single head of the household who has no means of support. The eligibility standards, requirements for applying, and the amount you receive, vary across the country. A few states pay benefits to the mother before the baby's birth, but many don't.

Married couples can't apply for this program. That doesn't mean that financial pressures don't exist for you. Frequently young marrieds said that this was one of their biggest obstacles. They'd never had to think about stretching paychecks, balancing budgets, let along trying to save for the future. Arguments about money matters might arise.

Married or single, you could qualify for food stamps. This is another federal program available in most cities. If you receive them, they might at least put a dent in your eating expenses. These are coupons issued by the government and accepted at most grocery stores. In a few locations only certain food commodities are offered. It's hard to provide a balanced diet for your family with just these products, but it's better than nothing. Again, the application procedures and the dollar values vary. Remember, for exact information about AFDC and food stamps you should contact the department of social services.

Peter and Tracy, who have been married for three years, are representative of many teen parents. Peter said, "We didn't really have a chance to get to know each other before the baby came. Other couples have one or two years—we had four months. We started fighting about things we'd never even considered. And money's always been a biggie."

Tracy briefly interrupted and explained, "It costs a fortune for baby stuff. Food stamps have helped, but eating is just a small part. Think about a crib, mattress, potty, blankets, maybe some toys. Clothing costs are enormous. It's $12 for a pair of jeans and he grows out of everything so fast. Then add in our rent, doctor bills, and you just don't have anything left over."

Recently Peter found a union job. For the first time they feel their major struggles are behind them. When Peter left the room, Tracy told me, "We may be the fairy tale case. We've got a beautiful baby and I've a beautiful husband. Our arguments still happen, but we've never fought in front of our child. We try to run a smooth ship and I think we do. Also, you have to be truly in love . . . and we are."

Single parents sometimes wish they were married. Married parents sometimes wish they were single. Single mothers worry that every man they date is scared that they are out "husband hunting." Some of those who are married succumb to all the additional pressures brought on by their youth, employment problems, thoughts that "life is passing them by," and file for divorce.

There was no firm agreement on which is easier—being married or single. If you make up your mind you want to succeed, that possibility increases. When problems seem insurmountable, the best advice is to ask for help—from friends, family, or professionals in the community.

For all parents, day care may become another issue. While raising a child is a full-time job, no one pays you a decent salary. For that reason you may discover you need other employment. Others of you may want to continue your schooling to improve your job opportunities. More recognize the benefit of quality time rather than quantity time with their child. You need moments alone, and your child benefits from being with other kids.

Unless you have some kind person who volunteers to watch your baby, finding suitable day care is one of the most difficult tasks to face. Reasonably-priced or free programs, if they exist, often have long waiting lists. Others require that the child be a certain age.

Cathy is sixteen and lives in Massachusetts. She wanted the best for her child. Her husband's salary didn't cover all their expenses. Daily she sifted through the newspaper classified ads. She went to her state employment agency for advice. When she eventually came up with a few leads, her problems multiplied.

She described her situation, "I couldn't apply for a job bouncing a kid on my knee. My aunt said she would watch him, but not forever. One problem down. Then I had to find someone to hire me, a high school dropout.

"That took time, but I finally got work. They weren't at all happy when I mentioned I had a child. They wanted to know what 'arrangements' I'd made for day care. They said I'd probably have a crummy attendance record, because babies get sick and I'd have to stay home. I told them everything was covered. Another problem taken care of.

"Getting work is simple compared to finding day care. The first place I called wouldn't accept kids that aren't potty-trained. James is just six weeks old. I've got months before that happens. Another place charged $40 a week! I'd end up broke if I sent him there. Each call got me more frustrated and burned. No one seemed willing to let me help myself.

"There was one place that seemed great, but they only let you use the nursery if you were in school. I can't afford to think about my education. A couple days ago I heard about PAGE—Pregnant Adolescent Girls Education. They turned me onto a center that takes babies as young as one month. I have to spend some time at the center, but I think I can juggle it all. There are doctors and others in case of difficulties. Things are finally looking up."

When Irene and I talked together we discussed these issues and more. One book can't prepare you for all aspects of being a young parent. Child abuse. Discipline techniques. Budgeting. Internal conflicts. All these could be covered, but time and space won't permit it. For the thousands of words that have been written and spoken on teen pregnancies, Irene wanted to include this final thought. She stressed, "Yes, for most of us we originally didn't want to be pregnant. But there's a big difference between an unplanned and an unwanted baby. In our society we use the phrase 'unwanted teenage pregnancies.' I don't like that.

"I think I speak for the majority of young parents —maybe the pregnancy wasn't intended, but now that we are raising our children they are very much wanted, desired, and adored. Anything that creates such happiness requires a degree of suffering and pain. That's what it's like being a parent."

We're back at the beginning of the circle. You've read about the larger meanings of teen sexual activity and the possible consequences of unintended pregnancies. It's up to you to make decisions that are comfortable and right. Don't allow yourself to be trapped on the treadmill of becoming a statistic. If you're convinced you are ready to handle a sexual relationship, learn about birth control and select the best method for you. Then use it conscientiously and consistently. If you don't want sex yet, don't do it just to keep up with others.

Love, pregnancy, and children can be your greatest joy. They can also bring your greatest heartbreak. The choice is yours.

BIBLIOGRAPHY

The Alan Guttmacher Institute. Research and Development Division of Planned Parenthood Federation of America. "11 Million Teenagers: What Can Be Done About the Epidemic of Adolescent Pregnancies in the United States." New York: 1976.

Ashdown-Sharp, Patricia. *A Guide to Pregnancy and Parenthood for Women on Their Own.* New York: Vintage Books, 1975.

Bernstein, Rose. *Helping Unmarried Mothers.* New York: Association Press, 1971.

Cain, Arthur H. *Young People and Sex.* New York: John Day Co., 1967.

Furstenberg, Frank. *Unplanned Parenthood: The Social Consequences of Teenage Childbearing.* New York: Macmillan, 1975.

Howard, Marion. *Only Human: Teenage Pregnancy and Parenthood.* New York: The Seabury Press, 1975.

Klerman, Lorraine and James Jekel. *School-age Mothers: Problems, Programs and Policies.* Camden, Conn.: Lennet Books, 1973.

Klibanoff, Susan and Elton. *Let's Talk About Adoption.* Boston: Little, Brown & Co., 1973.

Lindemann, Constance. *Birth Control and Unmarried Young Women.* New York: Springer Publishing Co., 1974.

Luker, Kristin. *Taking Chances: Abortion and the Decision not to Contracept.* Berkeley, Ca.: University of California Press, 1975.

Maxtone-Graham, Katrina. *Pregnant by Mistake: The Stories of Seventeen Women.* New York: Liveright, 1973.

Pannor, Reuben. *The Unmarried Father: New Approaches for Unmarried Parents.* New York: Springer Publishing Co., 1971.

Pierce, Ruth. *Single and Pregnant.* Boston: Beacon Press, 1970.

Rains, Prudence. *Becoming an Unwed Mother.* Chicago: Aldine Publishing Co., 1971.

Shapiro, Deborah. *Agencies and Foster Children.* New York: Columbia University Press, 1976.

Sorenson, Robert. *Adolescent Sexuality in Contemporary America.* New York: World Publishers, 1973.

Whelan, Elizabeth. *Making Sense Out of Sex.* New York: McGraw-Hill Publishing Co., 1975.

Zakler, Jack and Wayne Brandstadt. *The Teenage Pregnant Girl.* Springfield, Ill.: Charles Thomas Publishing Co., 1975.

INDEX

Florence Crittenton
League, 81–82
Foam, contraceptive, 32,
34
Food stamps, 19, 103
Foster care, 41, 84–87, 89
Furstenberg, Frank, Jr., 22,
48, 50

Gaston, Caroline, 74–75
Gestation, 46
Glick, Paul, 49
Grote, Barbara, 32
Guilt, 61
Guttmacher, Alan, Foundation, 16, 29

Hamilton, Gordon, 145
Hardy, Janet, 46–47
Headaches, 35
Health centers, 26, 29, 30
Heathens, 4, 5–6
High school health programs, 26–27
Homosexuality, 27
Hypertension, 45

Ignorance, 24–25, 37, 51
Independence, seeking,
35, 36
Information. See Sex education
Initiation rites, 6–7
Instillation method, 60
Insurance, 49, 71–72

Intercourse. See Sexual
intercourse
Internal examinations, 58
Intrauterine device
(I.U.D.), 34
IQ tests, 25, 47

Jackson, Jesse, 27
Jelly, contraceptive, 32, 34

Kantner, John, 34, 36, 48

Labor, 45
Lamaze method, 77
Loneliness, 35
Love, seeking, 2, 36

Marriage, 4, 6–10, 14, 17,
41, 47, 49–53, 103–106
Masturbation, 6, 8, 9, 27
Maternity homes, 81–84
Maturity, 2, 35
Media, 21–22
Medicaid program, 56–57,
71–72
Medical history, 58
Medication, 60
Menstruation, 10–11, 24,
28, 32, 39, 40
Midwives, 67
Miller, Warren, 32
Mills, Karen, 49
Minorities, 17–18, 50, 85
Miscarriages, 11, 16, 17,
34, 45–46, 60

ABOUT THE AUTHOR

Janet Bode has lived and worked in the United States, Europe, and Mexico. After receiving a degree in English from the University of Maryland she taught school, served as a community organizer, and was a public relations/program director. Then she concentrated on a writing career.

Her previous major publications include *View From Another Closet* and a book for adult readers about rape, *Fighting Back* as well as a young adult title on the subject for Franklin Watts: *Rape: Preventing It: Coping with the Medical, Legal, and Emotional Aftermath*. She has appeared on numerous radio and television programs, spoken before civic groups, and was an active participant with an anti-rape organization. The author resides in San Francisco.

**ROCHESTER
HIGH SCHOOL**